What Can I Do Now?

Music

Books in the
What Can I Do Now? Series

Art
Computers
Engineering, Second Edition
Fashion
Health Care
Music
Nursing, Second Edition
Radio and Television, Second Edition
Safety and Security, Second Edition
Sports, Second Edition

What Can I Do Now?

Music

Ferguson
An imprint of Infobase Publishing

What Can I Do Now? Music

Ferguson
An imprint of Infobase Publishing
132 West 31st Street
New York NY 10001

ISBN-10: 0-8160-6033-9
ISBN-13: 978-0-8160-6033-7

Library of Congress Cataloging-in-Publication Data

What can I do now? : Music.
     p. cm.
 Includes index.
 ISBN 0-8160-6033-9 (hc : alk. paper)
 1. Music—Vocational guidance. 2. Music trade—Vocational guidance.
 I. J.G. Ferguson Publishing Company. II. Title: Music.
 ML3795.W455 2007
 780.23—dc22   2006030644

Ferguson books are available at special discounts when purchased in bulk quantities for businesses, associations, institutions, or sales promotions. Please call our Special Sales Department in New York at (212) 967-8800 or (800) 322-8755.

You can find Ferguson on the World Wide Web at http://www.fergpubco.com

Text design by Kerry Casey
Cover design by Takeshi Takahashi

Printed in the United States of America

VB Hermitage 10 9 8 7 6 5 4 3 2 1

This book is printed on acid-free paper.

All links and Web addresses were checked and verified to be correct at the time of publication. Because of the dynamic nature of the Web, some addresses and links may have changed since publication and may no longer be valid.

Contents

Introduction

If you are considering a career in music—which presumably you are since you're reading this book—you must realize that the better informed you are from the start, the better your chances of having a successful, satisfying career.

There is absolutely no reason to wait until you get out of high school to "get serious" about a career. That doesn't mean you have to make a firm, undying commitment right now. One of the biggest fears most people face at some point (sometimes more than once) is choosing the right career, and frankly, many people don't "choose" at all. They take a job because they need one, and all of a sudden 10 years have gone by and they wonder why they're stuck doing something they hate. Don't be one of those people! You have the opportunity right now—while you're still in high school and still relatively unencumbered with major adult responsibilities—to explore, to experience, to try out a work path, or several paths if you're one of those overachieving types. Wouldn't you really rather find out sooner than later that you're not cut out to be a musician after all, that you'd actually prefer to be an audio recording engineer? Or a music therapist? Or a music librarian?

There are many ways to explore the music industry. What we've tried to do in this book is give you an idea of some of your options. The chapter "What Do I Need to Know about the Music Industry" will give you an overview of the field: a little history, where it's at today, and promises of the future; as well as a breakdown of its structure, how it's organized, and a glimpse of some of its many career options.

The Careers section includes 10 chapters, each describing in detail a specific music specialty: artist and repertoire executive, audio recording engineer, music conductor and director, musician, music librarian, music producer, music teacher, music therapist, music video director and producer, and songwriter. The educational requirements for these specialties range from high school diploma to master's degree. Those interested in performing careers will find that musical talent is often more important than formal education. These chapters rely heavily on firsthand accounts from real people on the job. They'll tell you what skills you need, what personal qualities you have to have, what the ups and downs of the jobs are. You'll also find out about educational requirements—including specific high school and college classes—advancement possibilities, related jobs, salary ranges, and the future outlook.

In keeping with the secondary theme of this book (the primary theme being "you can do something now"), Section 3: Do It Yourself urges you to take charge and start your own programs and activities where none exist. Why not?

The real meat of the book is in Section 4: What Can I Do Right Now? This is where you get busy and DO SOMETHING. The chapter "Get Involved: A Directory of Camps, Programs, and Competitions." will clue you in on the obvious volunteer and intern positions, the not-so-obvious summer camps and summer college study, competitions, and other opportunities.

While we think the best way to explore music is to jump right in and start doing it, there are plenty of other ways to get into the music mind-set. "Surf the Web" offers you a short annotated list of music-related Web sites where you can explore everything from job listings (start getting an idea of what employers are looking for now), to educational and certification requirements, to on-the-job accounts.

"Read a Book" is an annotated bibliography of books (some new, some old) and periodicals. If you're even remotely considering a career in music, reading a few books and checking out a few magazines is the easiest thing you can do. Don't stop with our list. Ask your librarian to point you to more music-related materials. Keep reading!

"Ask for Money" is a sampling of music scholarships. You need to be familiar with these because you're going to need money for school. You have to actively pursue scholarships; no one is going to come up to you in the hall one day and present you with a check because you're such a wonderful student. Applying for scholarships is work. It takes effort. It must be done right and, in many cases, it must be done a year in advance of when you need the money.

"Look to the Pros" is the final chapter. It's a list of professional organizations that you can turn to for more information about accredited schools, education requirements, career descriptions, salary information, job listings, scholarships, and much more. Time after time, professionals say that membership and active participation in a professional organization is one of the best ways to network (make valuable contacts) and gain recognition in your field.

High school can be a lot of fun. There are dances and football games; maybe you're in band or play a sport. Great! Maybe you hate school and are just biding your time until you graduate. That's too bad. Whoever you are, though, take a minute and try to imagine your life 5 years from now, 10 years from now. Where will you be? What will you be doing? Whether you realize it or not, how you choose to spend your time now—studying, playing, watching TV, working at a fast food restaurant, hanging out, whatever—will have an impact on your future. Take a look at how you're spending your time now and ask yourself, "Where is this getting me?" If you can't come up with an answer, it's probably "nowhere." The choice is yours. No one is going to take you by the hand and lead you in the "right" direction. It's up to you. It's your life. You can do something about it right now!

SECTION 1

What Do I Need to Know About Music?

From the catchy pop song blasting from your car radio, to timeless classical compositions by Mozart performed by a symphony, to the exhilarating musical theater production of *Rent,* and much more, music surrounds us in almost every part of our lives. If you love music, there is a career for you in this exciting and rewarding field—whether it is performing before screaming fans in a rock club, conducting an orchestra, organizing sheet music and other music-related materials in a music library, using music to help treat an emotionally disturbed child, teaching a young child to play the piano, writing about music for a magazine, or working in countless other settings. Read on for more information about the world of music!

GENERAL INFORMATION

Throughout human history, there have been numerous theories about how music originated. The great naturalist Charles Darwin thought that music was related to sex. In his view, music evolved from the mating cries of birds and animals. Others have proposed that early humans developed singing as a way of imitating the sounds of nature or communicating over distances longer than those over which simple speech could travel. The philosopher Suzanne Langer has speculated that music, language, and dance not only were used together but also developed together in early rituals that combined those activities in a kind of early opera. In fact, however, no one knows how or when music developed.

Music was an essential element in many early cultures and civilizations. It is known, for example, that Egyptians used music in various ways. Egyptian priests played seven-foot-tall harps in their temples to honor the gods; and Egyptian armies were accompanied by drums and trumpets, instruments that have accompanied warriors in many parts of the world. It was held that the god Osiris had invented the trumpet, and for that reason trumpets were used in rites dedicated to him.

Music was also extremely important to the early Hebrews, Assyrians, and Babylonians. The first important instrument in their part of the world was the kinnor, a triangular harp that had between 10 and 20 strings. It is said that solo performers as well as group performers in huge temple ceremonies used it. Reed flutes and drums of various kinds were also common. The shofar, a trumpet made of a ram's horn, is particularly well known among Jews and Christians because, according to the Old Testament, seven shofars were used by the Jews to knock down the walls of the fortress of Jericho. The shofar is still used in Jewish temples.

In music as well as in politics, philosophy, and science, the Greeks have influenced Western civilization. The very word *music* has Greek roots, although it should be noted that what the Greeks called music included all of what are now called the liberal arts. Although we do not know what the music of the ancient Greeks sounded like, various Greek concepts live on in modern Western music. The names of the various modes in Western music are taken directly from the names of the modes used by the Greeks, such as Ionian, Dorian, Phrygian, and Lydian. The Greeks also developed a system of notation so that their music could be written down and remembered. Unfortunately, however, scholars have not been able to decipher that notation with any degree of accuracy.

In the West, music was strongly influenced by the Roman Catholic Church. In fact, in the medieval period, the only places where formal musical education could be found were the Church's song schools, which trained boys to sing in religious services. The music that those boys sang was called plainsong, plainchant, or Gregorian chant. The music, which had developed from true chanting, featured simple melodies that used specific scales, or modes, that were authorized by the Church. As the years passed, more scales were authorized and the music became more complex. Ultimately, polyphony, the combination of two or more melodies, came to occupy a dominant place in Christian music until the Renaissance had almost run its course.

During the Renaissance, which ran roughly from 1400 to 1600, the mass and the motet were the primary musical forms, but secular forms such as the German lied, the English madrigal, and the French chanson were also widely used, as were various dance forms. Renaissance composers had little knowledge of how to combine instruments for best effect. Instrumental music became more important during the Renaissance, but composers still generally wrote for instruments

---

Lingo to Learn

acoustic Music that is not electronically enhanced.

amplifier An electronic component used to increase volume.

audition A trial performance that is used to test a musician's suitability for a performing job.

composition A piece of music written and arranged by a composer.

concerto A musical form in which the orchestra accompanies a solo instrument.

counterpoint The simultaneous use of more than one melody (note that counterpoint and polyphony have the same meaning).

demo An inexpensively produced recording that demonstrates a musician's ability.

discography A complete list of the recordings of a performer or producer.

genre A category of music, i.e. rap, country, rock, jazz.

gig A musical performance, usually live.

harmony The sonic phenomenon that occurs when more than one note is played or sung at once, resulting in a chord or some other harmonic structure.

improvisation Creating music on the spot, as opposed to performing music that was composed previously; sometimes called spontaneous composition.

key A scale that provides the harmonic material for a piece of music (a piece of music that is based on the C-major scale, for example, is said to be "in the key" of C major).

much as they wrote for voices, without taking into account the unique qualities of those instruments.

It was during the Baroque period (1600-1750) that instrumental composition truly came into its own, advanced by the efforts of such great composers as Johann Sebastian Bach, Georg Friedrich Handel, and Antonio Vivaldi. Harmony, which occurs when two or more notes are played or sung at once, took on new importance. The harmony that had existed during the Renaissance had been primarily unintentional, resulting when the simultaneous use of two or more melodies caused more than one note to be played or sung at once, but during the Baroque period composers manipulated harmony to achieve various musical effects. This rich musical era also saw the development of many musical forms, including the oratorio, cantata, aria, concerto, fugue, suite, sonata, and the prelude.

One of the most important developments in Western music, the creation of the opera, took place during the Baroque period. The opera is an art form that combines theater and orchestral music. In the early years of opera's existence (from about 1600), there were many kinds of operas, but with the passage of time the form became relatively standardized.

At the time of the early operas, the orchestra generally consisted of whichever instruments were available. By about 1700, however, various effective combinations of instruments had been determined, and by 1800 the orchestra had taken its modern form, which involves the grouping of similar instruments into sections, such as the brass section, the woodwind section, the string section, and the percussion section. The sections are positioned in such a way as to make the music as clear and as effective as possible.

The Classical movement in Western music began in approximately 1750 and ended by 1820. Its primary exponents were Wolfgang Amadeus Mozart, Joseph Haydn, Franz Schubert in his early period, and Ludwig van Beethoven in his early period. The Classical movement was characterized by formalism, simplicity, restraint, and little overt expression of emotion.

Composers who were part of the Romantic movement (1820-1900) rejected the restraint and formalism of the Classical composers and wrote music that attempted to express emotions in a direct manner. Among the foremost exponents of Romanticism were Franz Liszt, Richard Wagner, Johannes Brahms, and Pyotr Ilich Tchaikovsky. In addition, the later works of Beethoven and Schubert are considered Romantic.

By the end of the 19th century, the French composer Claude Debussy had begun composing works that came to be called Impressionistic, a term that had originally been used to describe the work of French painters such as Claude Monet and Edouard Manet. The general idea of the Impressionist painters was to avoid detail and paint what a person might see at a quick glance. In effect, this meant focusing on the play of light as it hit objects rather than on the shapes of the objects themselves. Debussy's compositions worked in a similar way, focusing on musical color and creating impressions that seemed to some listeners of the day indistinct and unfocused.

Although various movements existed in the late 19th century and the early 20th century, it is difficult to view 20th- and early 21st-century music in terms of distinct movements. While many 20th- and early 21st-century composers have attempted to find new sounds and harmonies (such as those resulting from the serial compositional techniques developed by the Viennese composer Arnold Schoenberg), many others have worked in one or more of the traditions that existed in earlier times.

STRUCTURE OF THE INDUSTRY

There is no single structure to the music industry, which consists of dozens of offshoots such as music performance; the music and recording industry; educational settings (musical schools, college departments of music, and home lessons); radio, television, and film; the Internet; cultural organizations; the health care industry (music therapists); the publishing industry (music journalists, composers); and libraries (music librarians), to name a few. One of the key relationships among these groups is between the artist or band and the music and recording industry. The following paragraphs detail this relationship and the steps that the music and recording industry take to identify and sign talent, create a recording, and market it to the public.

The recording industry is constantly on the lookout for new talent, new sounds, and new styles. *Music producers* and *artist and repertoire (A&R) executives* are responsible for finding the new talent and arranging the contract negotiations for a recording contract. They keep track of the musicians who are performing in clubs and concerts. They also keep in touch with the recording artists who are well known.

A representative of a record company either approaches a prospective new artist, or the artist sends in a three- to four-song demo tape to the A&R department of one or more companies. If the representative is interested in the artist's work, arrangements are then made between the company and the artist or the artist's manager. The contract may be for a single recording or a series of recordings.

For relatively unknown artists, an independent label is the most likely place to arrange a contract. The A&R staff for independent labels is most active in finding and representing artists or less-mainstream types of music. Multiple release contracts are common for independent labels, and if the artist becomes extremely popular, a major record label may buy out the contract. The independent label promotes albums to a lesser degree, and, for the smallest labels, the artist may be responsible for all album promotion. In rock, jazz, country, and rap music, many currently successful artists began on independent labels. In the last decade, to avoid buying-out expensive contracts for bands on independent labels, many of the major labels now have smaller subsidiaries that seek out progressive, up-and-coming artists, who, once they have reached a certain level of success on the subsidiary label, will make a smooth transition to the major label.

For the established performer or group, contract negotiations may be carried out between several companies vying for rights to publish the performers' work. Musicians generally benefit as each company tries to make the best offer.

Once the contract arrangements have been settled, the process of recording an album can begin. The artist and the music producer assigned to the artist decide the songs that are to be recorded. Artists on a major label may have to compromise their music to fit mainstream music tastes closely observed by industry executives. Independent labels generally allow musicians to record whatever they want and often encourage experimentation. The record producer hires studio musicians, recording technicians, and support staff.

During a recording session, more than one recording is made of the same song. With each recording, audio recording engineers vary input levels, microphone placement, and other factors that affect the recorded sound. The best sections from each version of the song can be put (or spliced) together for the best result. Each instrument and voice can be recorded separately onto its own track and combined later by recording engineers, who specialize in mixing different recorded sounds into a unified whole. Mixing the recording is one of the most important jobs performed in the production of a recording and can influence the sound as much as the musicians can.

For popular music, *recording engineers* use their tools of recording in a variety of ways to influence sound or to create entirely new sounds. Especially with current computer-aided recording and manipulation equipment, engineers and producers have increased control over the final sound, mood, and intensity of a recording. Recording engineers can change the sound of individual instruments, speed up or slow down tempo, correct missed or skipped beats, edit out unwanted sections and splice in new sections, and perform numerous other tasks in preparing the final version of a recording.

To record a live performance, the technical end is just as important, but the performer only has one shot at the recording. After the performance, the engineer can work with the different tracks of tape to edit flaws and outside noises and juggle with the volume and intensity to smooth over rough patches in the performance.

One of the most important aspects to the recording of a live performance is the position of the microphones. The location of microphones for a symphony determines the strength of the different sections of the orchestra. If solo performers are to be heard, individual microphones may be assigned to their positions on the stage. To maintain a balanced sound in the reproduction of a large performance such as a symphony, the sound recording technician's goal is to match the recorded sound with the balance that is achieved for the audience sitting in an orchestral hall.

Once the recording is finished and the album put together, or mastered, the production department takes over. This department is responsible for producing the actual recording in CD, cassette, and occasionally vinyl versions. The press run (the total number of releases produced) is determined by previous sales of the artist, and the anticipated increase or decrease in sales for the release. For new musicians, labels establish a new artist press run ranging from 1,000 to 10,000 copies. The A&R and promotion departments are responsible for knowing the market and the estimated value of a recording. Re-pressing a recording that is selling well is an easy process once the master tape is made.

While the album is in production, the art department is producing cover art and inside art if there is any. Type design is chosen for all written matter. Various designs are presented to the company representative, the artists, and the record producer for approval. For smaller companies, the artists may make all the final decisions on art and packaging. A final design is selected and then completed by the artists. For reissued albums, the art department may decide on its own which design to use on the cover. Musicians on independent labels are often responsible for creating their own artwork.

The marketing department of the record company creates the ads that will run in music magazines, on the radio, on the Internet, and on television for each album produced. Posters, show cards, displays, and any other promotional material are designed and developed in the advertising department as well. Advertising can greatly enhance sales of an album by generating an interest in the album either before its release or after it has been moved into the stores.

One of the chief methods of generating interest in a release is airplay on the radio. The promotions department is expected to keep up-to-date on the staff and audience of radio stations. They should be aware of which audiences are covered in each region of the country and how to best promote the new product to the audience interested in that type of music.

In the past decade, the Internet has also become a key tool in advertising and promoting musical acts. Most record companies have Web sites that list information about their artists, play music videos, and provide free downloads to generate interest in a new album or new act. Most companies also sell electronic, downloadable versions of their songs and albums online.

Just as important, or possibly even more important than radio play or Internet advertising for commercially successful rock, country, and rap music today, is having a music video broadcast, particularly on MTV or VH1—the two major music video stations. Producers and musicians contact video directors and discuss concepts for an original video. Often the musicians act in the video, or professional actors are hired to play roles.

The promotions and publicity department is responsible for sending out copies of the recording to reviewers, along with press kits providing information and photos of the artist. This press package is mainly geared toward the airplay time that can be generated by favorable reviews and frequent audience requests to the radio station. Other forms of publicity used to create an interest in the recording include concert performances, interviews on television and radio, press coverage in the printed media, public appearances, and any other promotion that brings the artist into the public eye.

Once album sales are underway, determining the success or failure of a recording is directly linked to the number of recordings sold. For a successful classical album, the number sold may be 5,000 to 10,000 copies. For a popular music album, the numbers are more likely to approach or exceed one million copies. Well-known performers regularly have record sales that exceed one million copies. After the record is sold, the recording may be re-released or may go out of print. Sales of most albums decline quickly after release and may not need a second pressing. Some albums, however, may be marketed successfully for years.

CAREERS

Musicians are the most recognizable workers in the music industry. There are many kinds of musicians, but some of the largest categories are: *instrumentalists* (those who play instruments), *singers, conductors, composers, songwriters, arrangers, orchestrators, copyists,* and *teachers.*

Musicians play many kinds of instruments, but those instruments usually fall into specific categories. String instruments produce sound when their strings are either plucked or strummed, as is the case with the guitar and the mandolin, or bowed, as is the case with the cello, the viola, and the violin. Wind instruments, or woodwinds, produce sound when air is blown through them, as do brass instruments, which are sometimes called brasswinds. Some woodwinds have mouthpieces equipped with reeds. When the player blows through the mouthpiece, the reed vibrates, producing sound. Instruments such as clarinets and saxophones use a single reed, whereas instruments such as oboes and bassoons are equipped with double reeds. The flute, however, does not use reeds at all. Instead, it produces sound when a player blows air at an angle against a fixed mouthpiece. Brass instruments also generally have a fixed mouthpiece. Percussion instruments, such as drums, produce sound when they are struck by a hand or by an object such as a stick or a mallet. The piano, which produces sound when its strings are struck by hammers that are activated when a pianist presses the piano's keys, is also considered a percussion instrument.

Singers use their voices to make music. In most cases, singers sing words, or lyrics, that are intended to match the music accompanying them. In some cases, however, singers use their voices as instruments. In Western classical music, singing without words is called vocalization. In jazz, some singers use a technique called *scat singing*, which involves using sounds in place of words.

Conductors "play" an orchestra, choir, or other ensemble rather than an instrument. It is the job of the conductor to ensure, among other things, that the musicians play the correct notes at the correct times, that instruments or voices start and stop at the right times, that instruments and voices are neither too loud nor too soft and are in balance with one another, that the music being performed is interpreted in an appropriate manner (which usually means honoring the composer's intentions), and that the music has an impact—usually an emotional impact—on the listeners. Conductors must know the music they are conducting inside and out, which means that much time must be spent in preparation before the conductor works with the ensemble. Conductors use their hands or a baton to indicate the basic rhythm that is being played by the ensemble, which helps the musicians to keep together. Conducting is a demanding profession that requires a very high level of knowledge, expertise, sensitivity, and intuition.

A musical composer is a person who creates original music. Some composers, such as those who write orchestral music, write their music using notation, which ensures that musicians who can read notation can play their music. In the case of classical music, the written music that results is very detailed. Some recording artists who are composers create music by giving oral or other nonwritten instructions to their musicians, using no notation whatsoever, yet the pieces they create are considered compositions. Many songwriters (composers who specialize in the song form) who record their songs give their musicians a lead sheet that consists of a melody and a set of chord changes, which gives the musicians basic instructions yet also allows them the freedom to interpret the music in specific ways of their own choosing. In many cases, composers or songwriters who do not read music and cannot write notation hire formally trained musicians to write down their songs, so that others can use the written music. Songwriters may write both music and lyrics or may write one or the other exclusively. Those who do not write lyrics work with a lyricist, who provides the words.

Arrangers generally create a musical background for a preexisting melody. An arranger may create an introduction and a coda (ending) for a melody as well as add countermelodies (additional melodies) to the original melody. In effect, the arranger composes additional material that was not provided by the original composer and ensures that the background sets off the original melody in an effective manner. An orchestrator takes a piece of music, perhaps one that already has a basic arrangement, and assigns the parts to specific instruments in the orchestra or other ensemble. For this reason, the orchestrator must have a tremendous amount of knowledge regarding exactly what the various instruments can and cannot do. An orchestrator may decide, for example, that a particular melody should be played by a solo flute or by a flute and an oboe, so that a very specific sound will be achieved. An orchestrator must also know how to notate parts for various instruments. All the choices that the orchestrator makes will have a significant impact on

---

More Lingo to Learn

lyrics   The words of a song.

MIDI   Acronym for musical instrument digital interface; allows for the connection of musical instruments and computers.

mix   To blend tracks electronically for a recording.

mode   A scale that results when the notes of a given scale are played in one of a number of possible orders.

reverb   Sound created by many reflections in a small space.

scale   A particular set of notes arranged in an ascending or descending order.

session   The time spent in a recording studio.

sonata   A musical form that contains the following three sections exposition, development, and recapitulation (musical material is introduced and displayed in the exposition section, developed in the development section, and revisited in the recapitulation section).

studio musician   A musician who earns a living by playing music that is recorded in a recording studio.

tempo   Italian for speed; the speed at which a piece of music is played.

timbre   The particular quality of sound of a voice or instrument.

track   A band of recorded sound on magnetic tape.

twelve-tone composition (also **dodecaphonic or serial composition**)   The technique of using the 12 tones of Western music, arranged in an unchangeable order selected by the composer, as the sole source of a composition's melody, harmony, and counterpoint.

world music   Ethnic music or music that has been influenced by ethnic music.

---

the way the music will sound. Arranging and orchestrating are very closely related, and many professionals perform both tasks. Many composers also do their own arranging and orchestrating.

Copyists take the rough drafts of written music provided by composers, arrangers, or orchestrators and turn them into polished final products. Good copyists know how to determine the best way to write various passages of music in order to make them easily playable. As any

musician who has tried to read a poorly written piece of music knows, the job of the copyist is critical. A performance may be ruined by badly written music, especially when the musicians are playing music that they have not had a chance to rehearse sufficiently, which is often the case. A copyist may have to rewrite parts that have not been written correctly. If a composer has written a piece of music intended for harp as if it had been intended for piano, for example, the copyist will recast the music in the specific notation that harpists use. Many copyists work on computers, but some copyists still work by hand. The copying required for a large orchestral work typically costs thousands of dollars.

Many musicians are teachers. Some teach full time in institutions such as colleges, conservatories, high schools, and grade schools, while many others teach privately or run their own small teaching studios. Many teachers teach because they love teaching; for others, however, teaching supplements their meager performance income and enables them to survive.

NON-PERFORMANCE CAREERS

The following paragraphs detail non-performance careers in music.

In the artist and repertoire (A&R) department of a record company, *A&R coordinators, executives,* and other workers locate new talent and convince the company to sign them to contracts. A&R workers are also involved in producing their artists' CDs, promoting them, arranging concert tours, and other details of management.

Audio recording engineers oversee the technical end of recording. They operate the controls of the recording equipment—often under the direction of a music producer—during the production of music recordings; film, television, and radio productions; and other mediums that require sound recording.

An agent is a salesperson who sells artistic talent. *Music agents* act as the representatives for musical performers such as musicians, singers, orchestras, bands, and other musical groups, promoting their talent and managing legal contractual business. *Music scouts* search for musical talent at clubs, concert halls, and other music venues.

Music journalists report on the latest music releases and public performances of all genres. Their work appears in print and online newspapers and magazines, or is used in radio or television broadcasts. They work on periodical staffs or as freelance writers.

As prominent professionals in the information services field, librarians help others find information and select materials best suited to their needs. They are key personnel wherever books, magazines, audiovisual materials, and a variety of other informational materials are cataloged and kept. Librarians help make access to these reference materials possible. *Music librarians* perform many of the same duties as traditional librarians, but specialize in managing materials related to music.

Music producers are responsible for the overall production of commercially recorded music. They work closely with recording artists and audio recording engineers to ensure everything runs smoothly and according to plan during a recording session. They monitor and control the technical aspects of a session, such as microphone placement, tracks used, sound and effects, musician needs, and anything else that influences the quality of the recorded music, as well as see to other needs of the musicians and recording engineers. They review prospective new artists, maintain ties with contracted artists, and may negotiate contract and recording arrangements. They also work on the final mixing and editing of the recording.

Music therapists treat and rehabilitate people with mental, physical, and emotional disabilities. They use the creative process of music in their therapy sessions to determine the underlying causes of problems and to help patients achieve therapeutic goals. The specific objectives of the therapeutic activities vary according to the needs of the patient and the setting of the therapy program.

Music venue owners and managers are responsible for the overall success of a music venue. They book music acts, oversee employees, and play a role in the hiring and firing of staff. While owners have the final say in the club's business decisions, managers handle the daily operations of the venue, such as hiring, training, and scheduling staff members, planning music programming, checking music and bar equipment, and ensuring the safety and cleanliness of the club.

Music video directors are responsible for guiding actors, casting, costuming, cinematography, lighting, editing, and sound recording for music videos. Music video directors must have insight into the many tasks that go into the creation of a music video, and they must have a broad vision of how each part will contribute to the final product.

Music video editors perform an essential role in the music industry. They take an unedited draft of film or videotape and use specialized equipment to improve the draft until it is ready for viewing. It is the responsibility of the video editor to create the most effective product possible that reflects the intentions of the featured music artist—or more precisely, the artist's record label.

Music video producers often work with the music video director by overseeing the budget, production schedule, and

Listening Trends

Genre	Percentage of Buyers Who Purchased Genre in 2005
Rock	31.5
Country	12.5
Rap/Hip-Hop	13.3
R&B/Urban	10.2
Pop	8.1
Religious	5.3
Children's	2.3
Jazz	1.8
Classical	2.4
Oldies	1.1
Soundtracks	0.9
New Age	0.4
Other	8.5

Source: Recording Industry Association of America

other tasks associated with music video production.

Musical instrument repairers and tuners work on a variety of instruments, often operating inside music shops or repair shops to keep the pieces in tune and in proper condition. Those who specialize in working on pianos or pipe organs may travel to the instrument's location to work. Instrument repairers and tuners usually specialize in certain families of musical instruments, such as stringed or brass instruments. Depending on the instrument, they may be skilled in working with wood, metal, electronics, or other materials.

EMPLOYMENT OPPORTUNITIES

Generally speaking, musicians make money by playing in clubs, at concerts, at festivals, and by doing studio work. They also make and sell recordings, which is a major source of income. Some artists are primarily recording artists—in fact, some do not perform live at all—whereas others make most of their living by performing. The most popular of these performers also make music videos, which serve to publicize the musicians and, with luck, increase sales of their recordings.

Musicians are employed in many other settings. Some musicians work at resorts, on cruise ships, in gambling casinos, and at state fairs. Others play in wedding bands, while others work in churches, temples, schools, clubs, restaurants, in opera and ballet productions, and on film, television, and radio. The most talented musicians might play in a professional choir, symphony, or orchestra. In addition to performing, some musicians may also teach music or write about music for magazines and newspapers.

In most cases, musical performing careers do not last a lifetime. For every Stevie Wonder or Bruce Springsteen there are scores of once-prominent entertainers who have become businesspeople, managers, agents, or dropped out of the music business entirely. And for every one of the performers who has even briefly had a period of fame, there are thousands who never accomplish their goals in the arts. One thing that continues to attract the thousands of would-be musicians is the fame and fortune associated with the occupations. Indeed, the financial rewards that flow to famous musicians make them symbols of success alongside sports figures and industrialists. The great figures in music are admired and pointed out, not only because they are talented, but also because they are celebrities. Most artists, however, do not enjoy this fame.

In addition to careers in musical performance, there are many other rewarding opportunities in the music business. Many people with a love of music seek opportunities in the music and recording industry. Although four corporations—Universal Music Group, Warner Music Group, Sony, and EMI—control over 80 percent of the industry, there are countless independent labels—such as Bloodshot, Alligator, Matador, and Dischord—that provide opportunities to aspiring artist and repertoire workers, audio recording technicians and engineers, music producers, musicians, advertising workers, and clerical and support staff.

Others pursue music-related careers in journalism, health care, education, television and film, radio, publishing, the Internet, and in countless other settings.

INDUSTRY OUTLOOK

According to the *Occupational Outlook Handbook,* employment of musicians will increase about as fast as the average for all occupations through 2014. Religious organizations, where the majority of these workers are employed, will continue to offer the most new wage and salary jobs for musicians. Most openings will occur when musicians leave the field for other work because their earnings are so low, creating similar low-paying opportunities for up-and-coming musicians.

Because so many young people want to become musicians, competition is extremely intense in virtually all fields of music. Although extremely talented musicians have a better chance than others do of becoming successful, even those musicians have no guarantee of success. People skills, business knowledge, and a knack for self-promotion have become more and more important.

The recording industry is in a continual state of flux. New technology, new music, new markets, and new ways of doing business are constantly redefining the way the industry functions. Computer technology is simplifying the recording and mixing process while opening new outlets for creativity. Musicians, producers, and engineers are finding opportunities in the creation of music for Web sites and other multimedia. In addition, advances in technology have made it possible for musicians to buy or rent at a relatively low price the equipment they need to produce their own recordings. Many artists now sell their own recordings by direct mail and through the Internet, avoiding the large record companies and producers that pop musicians must court. Self-production ensures that artists can make their own creative decisions and pocket a higher percentage of their earnings than they would receive if they worked with record companies.

Outside the commercial mainstream, many artists have found that they can make a decent living by catering to small, devoted audiences. For example, music for children has enjoyed especially strong growth as singers and songwriters who once primarily focused on reaching adult audiences begin to market to this fast-growing demographic.

In the last decade the music and recording industry has undergone dramatic consolidation. As previously mentioned, now only four corporations—Universal Music Group, Warner Music Group, Sony, and EMI—control over 80 percent of the industry. While this consolidation may be beneficial for artists under contract with these companies, it has also made it more difficult for unknown acts to break into the business.

SECTION 2

Careers

Artist and Repertoire Executives

SUMMARY

Definition
In the artist and repertoire (A&R) department of a record company, A&R executives locate new talent and convince the company to sign them to contracts. A&R executives are also involved in producing their artists' CDs, promoting them, arranging concert tours, and other details of management.

Alternative Job Titles
Artist and repertoire coordinators
Artist and repertoire representatives
Recording industry executives

Salary Range
$20,000 to $85,000 to $200,000+

Educational Requirements
Bachelor's degree

Certification or Licensing
None available

Employment Outlook
About as fast as the average

High School Subjects
Business
Music
Speech

Personal Interests
Music
Selling/making a deal

Up until high school graduation, Joe Poindexter always intended on becoming a politician. But on the way to a career in this field, he discovered the music industry. "When I moved to Illinois for college," he recalls, "I was quickly immersed into the local music scene there and became intrigued about the stories and careers of the bands that had seen some success. After reading some literature about the music business and attending the CMJ festival in New York and the South by Southwest festival in Austin, I decided to give it a go. I have since learned that my interest in politics has come in quite handy, and the necessity to manage personalities (as successful politicians do with their constituents) is ever strong in the music business."

WHAT DOES AN ARTIST & REPERTOIRE EXECUTIVE DO?

If you're in a band, and you've tried to get some local, paying gigs, then you're familiar with how difficult it can be to get your music heard. You'll likely meet with even more frustration if you try to market your band nationally in an effort to get a record contract. *Artist and repertoire (A&R) executives* know firsthand the number of artists hoping to sign with a record label—thousands of submissions cross their desks every year.

A&R executives review these submissions, looking and listening for talented musicians. They listen to demo tape after demo tape, and read through press clippings and artist biographies. They also keep track of the music scene by attending clubs and reading fanzines. A&R executives visit Web sites and download samples. Although they listen to a lot of music that doesn't interest them, occasionally they come across something that stands out. When they do, A&R executives set out to get to know the artist better. Just because A&R executives like an artist's demo tape, it doesn't mean they will automatically sign the artist to a contract. They first have to get a complete sense of the artist's talents. They may request additional recorded songs and go to live performances. Once they feel confident about the artist's talent, A&R executives attempt to get him or her a record deal. This involves convincing other executives at the record company that the artist is worth the risk. But an A&R executive may also work with an artist that is being pursued by A&R representatives from other companies. In such cases, the A&R worker has to convince the artist that he or she will receive the attention and care he or she needs.

The work of A&R representatives doesn't end when they've signed the talent to a contract. A&R executives become closely involved in the careers of their artists. They help match them with producers and assist in the mixing of the tracks. They also help promote the artists—from helping them select the right clothes to wear for the CD cover photograph, to arranging interviews, to deciding which singles should be played on the radio. In many cases, A&R representatives work with artists closely throughout their careers, helping them to stay successful as artists and businesspeople.

Work with a record company can be very exciting—A&R executives have the opportunity to make decisions about what music people will be listening to and which artists will get a shot at success. The work can be very stressful and intense. A&R professionals work long hours, making phone calls, devising schedules, reviewing contracts, and handling many other details of management. They have to sort through a lot of bad music to find the few artists that interest them. They also devote many evenings to scouting out new talent at clubs.

WHAT IS IT LIKE TO BE AN ARTIST & REPERTOIRE EXECUTIVE?

Joe Poindexter has worked in the music industry for eight years—four of which have been as an A&R executive. "I started out as a college representative for the Universal Music Group at the University of Illinois in Champaign-Urbana," he says. "My first position in A&R was at Elementree Records, an imprint label of

Record Companies on the Web

A&M Records
http://www.amrecords.com

Alligator Records
http://www.alligator.com

American Recordings
http://www.americanrecordings.com

Atlantic Records
http://www.atlanticrecords.com

Bloodshot
http://www.bloodshotrecords.com

Capitol Records
http://www.hollywoodandvine.com

Columbia Records
http://www.columbiarecords.com

Def Jam Records
http://www.defjam.com

Dischord Records
http://www.dischord.com

EMI Music Group
http://www.emimusicpub.com

Epic Records
http://www.epiccenter.com

Flawless Records
http://www.flawless-records.com

Geffen Records
http://www.geffen.com

Hollywood Records
http://hollywoodrecords.go.com

Interscope Records
http://www.interscope.com

Island Records
http://www.islandrecords.com

J Records
http://www.jrecords.com

Jive Records
http://www.zombalabelgroup.com

Matador Records
http://www.matadorrecords.com

RCA Records
http://www.rcarecords.com

Reprise Records
http://www.repriserecords.com

Sire Records
http://www.sirerecords.com

SonyBMG
http://www.sonybmg.com

Universal Music Group
http://new.umusic.com

Virgin Records America
http://www.virginrecords.com

Warner Music Group
http://www.wmg.com

Geffen Records owned by Jonathan Davis of the rock band Korn. I'm now at Hollywood Records, a division of the Walt Disney Corporation. Hollywood Records is the home to such artists as Queen, Breaking Benjamin, Hilary Duff, and Los Lobos. I am currently working on records with Sparta and the Indigo Girls."

Joe says that his job varies from day to day. "One day," he says, "might be exclusively focused on taking meetings with managers/lawyers/producers and listening to demos that come in the mail. Another day might require me to be in the studio with a band that I signed, who are making their new record. Some days

To Be a Successful Artist and Repertoire Executive, You Should . . .

- be a good communicator
- have an excellent knowledge of the music industry
- have strong organization skills
- have an ear for talent
- be able to work well with a variety of people
- have an outgoing personality

require me to meet with other members of the record label staff, to make sure everything is in place for our campaign on an album I just made with a band I signed. And other days, I'm traveling and spending time with an artist that I am pursuing."

DO I HAVE WHAT IT TAKES TO BE AN ARTIST & REPERTOIRE EXECUTIVE?

To be a successful A&R executive, you'll need a love for music and an interest in the business end of the music industry. You should have a good sense of the history of popular music as well as the acts that are currently on the scene. You'll also need to be very organized; A&R executives for big companies generally must handle many different acts in different stages of production.

Joe says that personal values for A&R executives vary based on the individual's career goals and personality. "It all depends on what one is looking to get out of the music business," he explains. "If fame and fortune are what you seek, you need to be strong-minded and not afraid to go against anyone who might stand in the way of your road to success. If your goal is to make a good name for yourself and sign acts that you feel are important for the future of music, your set of values is completely different. Those who last the longest in the music business are generally a little bit of both of these character descriptions."

Working in the music industry is exciting, but those interested in the field need to be aware that this is a high-stress industry that demands results. "It is quite simple," Joe explains. "If you sign artists that are successful, being an A&R guy can afford you many luxuries. If you sign artists that cost the company a lot of money and don't perform all that well, you could be quickly out of a job. The most difficult thing to grasp is that anyone can be both of these in his or her career in A&R. You could have a great run for 5 to 10 years; but as with every business, it has to be about today and not yesterday. With that said, heads of record companies always want A&R people who are performing well *today*. Those that have had tremendous success in the past are just as vulnerable as the young kids just out of college who want to hustle their way to the top."

HOW DO I BECOME AN ARTIST & REPERTOIRE EXECUTIVE?

Education

High School

Most A&R executives have a college degree, so in high school you should pursue a college preparatory track. Classes in business, mathematics, speech, and English will be helpful. The most important thing you can do is to become involved in music, be it playing in a school band or with a group of friends, or simply listening to a wide variety of music in your spare time.

Postsecondary Training

Executives in the music industry come from a variety of backgrounds. You'll likely need a college degree, but experience with a record company will be the most valuable training. Some A&R executives have degrees in communications, business, marketing, and music.

Internships and Volunteerships

Some major record companies offer internship opportunities; check with your college's internship office for information. Although internships are often unpaid, they are excellent ways to break into this highly competitive industry. As an intern, you might answer phones, file paperwork, or perhaps even write a press release or participate in a marketing campaign to promote a new artist.

You may be able to find a volunteer opportunity at a very small record company, but opportunities are limited due to the competitive nature of the industry. If you can't locate an internship or a volunteer opportunity, you can still learn about the music industry by listening to a wide variety of music and following the careers of your favorite recording artists by reading magazines and surfing the Internet. You can also visit clubs that regularly book live music; some clubs host "all-ages" shows for young music lovers. If possible, join a group to learn about the challenges of performing with others, composing original music, booking gigs, and managing the business side of music.

WHO WILL HIRE ME?

There are hundreds of record companies across the country, but many are small, independent labels staffed by very few people. Four corporations—Universal Music Group, Warner Music Group, SonyBMG, and EMI—now control over 80 percent of the industry in the United States and employ the majority of A&R executives. Independent labels employ others. Most positions are located in Los Angeles, New York City, and Nashville.

Getting a job in A&R can be very difficult—such positions are highly sought after. After college, you can try to pursue an entry-level position with a record company. You should work in any department in which there's a job opening. Check the help wanted ads in such trade magazines as *Billboard* (http://www.billboard.com) and *Variety* (http://www.variety.com), or seek out temporary employment agencies that specialize in placing people in jobs in the entertainment industry. Once you get your foot in the door at a record company, you will have the opportunity to prove yourself and eventually work your way up into an A&R-related position.

WHERE CAN I GO FROM HERE?

Once A&R executives gain some experience in the music industry, whether within a company or as a freelance producer or manager, they will be able to make connections with other, more experienced A&R professionals. An A&R executive may begin as an assistant, then work up into a position as a coordinator, and later as a vice president or president of the department.

WHAT ARE THE SALARY RANGES?

A&R executives in entry-level positions make around $20,000 a year. More senior positions can pay upwards of $85,000. Experienced executives with major record companies can make more than $200,000 a year. Full-time employment with a record company usually includes health and retirement benefits, as well as bonuses.

WHAT IS THE JOB OUTLOOK?

The A&R worker will always be important to record companies, and positions

Related Jobs

- artist managers
- broadcasting executives
- entertainment lawyers
- music agents and scouts
- music producers
- musicians
- singers
- songwriters

within an A&R department will always be difficult to get. The work itself will be affected greatly by the Internet in the years to come. Already, A&R executives are surfing the Web for artists marketing themselves with their own Web sites. Technological advances have allowed for quick and easy downloading of music and other forms of media from the Internet, and some artists are now using the Web to bypass record companies entirely. So, in addition to competing with other record companies for talent, A&R executives may be competing with the artists themselves for the opportunity to distribute their music.

Audio Recording Engineers

SUMMARY

Definition
Audio recording engineers oversee the technical end of recording. They operate the controls of the recording equipment—often under the direction of a music producer—during the production of music recordings; film, television, and radio productions; and other mediums that require sound recording.

Alternative Job Titles
None

Salary Range
$19,460 to $44,130 to $82,610+

Educational Requirements
Some postsecondary training

Certification or Licensing
Recommended

Employment Outlook
About as fast as the average

High School Subjects
Computer science
Mathematics
Music
Shop (trade/vo-tech education)

Personal Interests
Computers
Figuring out how things work
Music

Recording engineer Steve Bellamy says that the greatest part of his job is working with talented musicians. "I recently did a CD recording for a musician who plays the cello," he recalls. "I have done many recordings with cellists, and most of them have been in a traditional classical setting. But every song on this album was unique and for each one the cellist was playing with very different musicians. One of the tunes featured a well-known DJ. Another featured a famous classical guitarist. A few weeks later, I recorded the same cello player live in concert with a jazz big-band in New York.

"Working in the audio field gives me so many opportunities to meet and work with musicians who are doing new and interesting things. I am around music all day long, and I also get to satisfy my interest in technology by using it to make recordings sound better. Sometimes the working hours can be very long and irregular, but most days I feel like I am making a living doing my hobby. I couldn't imagine working every day at something I didn't enjoy."

WHAT DOES AN AUDIO RECORDING ENGINEER DO?
Audio recording engineers operate and maintain the equipment used in a sound

To Be a Successful Audio Recording Engineer, You Should . . .

- have strong technical skills
- be a good communicator
- have patience
- be able to work well with a variety of people
- have excellent troubleshooting skills
- have an outgoing personality

recording studio. They record music, live and in studios; speech, such as dramatic readings of novels or radio advertisements; and sound effects and dialogue used in television and film. They work in control rooms at master console boards often containing hundreds of dials, switches, meters, and lights, which the engineer reads and adjusts to achieve desired results during a recording. Today, the recording studio is often considered an extra instrument, and thus, the audio recording engineer becomes an extra musician in his or her ability to dramatically alter the final sound of the recording.

As recording engineers prepare to record a session, they ask the musicians and producer what style of music they will be playing and what type of sound and emotion they want reflected in the final recording. Audio recording engineers must find out what types of instruments and orchestration will be recorded to determine how to manage the recording session and what additional equipment will be needed. For example, each instrument or vocalist may require a special microphone. The recording of dialogue will take considerably less preparation.

Before the recording session, audio recording engineers test all microphones, chords, recording equipment, and amplifiers to ensure everything is operating correctly. They load tape players and set recording levels. Many recording studios do not use tape anymore, but instead record directly to hard disc using a digital audio workstation. In this case, it is the engineer's responsibility to operate the computer software and ensure the integrity of the recorded sounds. Microphones must be positioned in precise locations near the instrument or amplifier. They experiment with several different positions of the microphone and listen in the control room for the best sound. Depending on the size of the studio and the number of musicians or vocalists, audio recording engineers position musicians in various arrangements to obtain the best sound for the production. For smaller projects, such as three- to eight-piece bands, each instrument may be sectioned off in soundproof rooms to ensure the sounds of one instrument do not "bleed" into the recording of another instrument. For more complex recording of larger orchestration, specialized microphones must be placed in exact locations to record one or several instruments.

Once audio recording engineers have the musicians in place and the microphones set, they instruct musicians to play a sample of their music. At the main console, they read the gauges and set recording levels for each instrument. Recording engineers must listen for sound imperfections, such as hissing, popping, "mike bleeding," and any other extraneous noises, and pinpoint their source. They turn console dials to adjust recording level, volume, tone, and effects. Depending on the problem, they may have to reposition either the microphone or the musician.

With the right sound and recording level of each microphone set, audio recording engineers prepare the recording equipment (either tape or digital). During the recording of a song or voice-over, they monitor the recording level of each microphone to ensure none of the tracks are too high, which results in distortion, or too low, which results in weak sound quality. Recording engineers usually record more than one "take" of a song. Before the mixing process, they listen to each take carefully and determine which one has the best sound. They often splice the best part of one take with the best part of another take.

In some recording sessions, two engineers work in the control room. One usually works with the recording equipment, and the other takes instruction from the producer. The engineers coordinate the ideas of the producer to create the desired sound. During each session, the volume, speed, intensity, and tone quality must be carefully monitored. Producers may delegate more responsibility to the recording engineer. Engineers often tell the musicians when to start and stop playing or when to redo a certain section. They may ask musicians or other studio technicians to move microphones or other equipment in the studio to improve sound quality.

After the recording is made, the individual tracks must be "mixed" to a master tape. When mixing, they balance each instrument in relation to the others. Together with the producer and the musicians, recording engineers listen to the song or piece several times with the instruments at different levels and decide on the best sound and consistency. At this stage, they also set equalization and manipulate sound, tone, intensity, effects, and speed of the recording. Mixing a record is often a tedious, time-consuming task that can take several weeks to complete, especially with some recordings of 24 or more tracks. At a larger studio, this may be done exclusively by a *sound mixer*. Sound mixers study various mixing methodologies.

Audio recording engineers frequently perform maintenance and repair on their equipment. They must identify and solve common technical problems in the studio. They may have to rewire or move equipment when updating the studio with new equipment. They may write proposals for equipment purchases and studio design changes. Apprentices, who are also known as studio technicians, often assist engineers in many of the basic sound recording tasks.

Recording engineers at smaller studios may set studio times for musicians. They must keep a thorough account of the band or performer scheduled to play, the musical style of the band or performer, the specific equipment that will be needed, and any other special arrangements needed to make the session run smoothly. They make sure the studio is stocked with the right, working accessory equipment, including chords, cables, microphones, amplifiers, tapes, tuners, and effect pedals.

Recording studios can be comfortable places to work. They are usually air conditioned because of the sensitivity of the equipment. They may be loud or cramped, however, especially during recording sessions where many people are working in a small space. The work is not particularly demanding physically (except when recording engineers must move equipment), but there may be related stress depending on the personalities of the producer and the performers. Audio recording engineers must be able to follow directions from producers and must often give directions. Their work must be quick and precise, and the engineer must be able to work as part of a team. Depending on the type of recording business, some engineers may be required to record off-site, at live concerts, for example, or other places where the recording is to take place. Engineers can usually come to work dressed however they wish.

Engineers must have patience when working with performers. For the engineer, there are often long periods of waiting while the musicians or performers work out problems and try to perfect parts of their songs. Engineers will frequently have to record the same song or spoken-word piece several times after mistakes have been made in the presentation. In addition, the mixing process itself can become tedious for many engineers—especially if they are not fond of the music. During the mix, engineers must listen to the same song over and over again to assure a proper balance of the musical tracks, and they often try various mixes.

Working hours depend on the job. Some studios are open at night or on the weekends to accommodate the schedules of musicians and performers. Other studios and recording companies only operate during normal business hours. Engineers work between 40 and 60 hours a week and may frequently put in 12-hour work days. Album or compact disc recordings typically take 300 to 500 hours each to record. In contrast, educational or language cassette recordings take only about 100 hours.

WHAT IS IT LIKE TO BE AN AUDIO RECORDING ENGINEER?

Steve Bellamy has been a recording engineer and educator for 11 years. For most of that time, he worked independently as a freelance recording engineer. In 2005, he accepted the position of senior recording engineer at The Banff Centre, which is a continuing education facility for artists, musicians, and recording engineers in Banff, Alberta, Canada. "I have always loved music," he says, "and I have always been interested in science. I played saxophone throughout high school and then did a bachelor of music degree, majoring in saxophone and in conducting/score study. During that time, I also played music in a couple of jazz and folk bands. As I approached the end of my studies, I wasn't sure which direction to take. I knew I wanted to be around music all the time, but I was pretty sure I didn't want the life of a full-time performer. I was actually visiting some friends in the jazz program at McGill University during the spring break of my final year of the BMus degree, and they told me that McGill offered a master's degree in sound recording. I thought it would be interesting to try this because it offered the chance to work with musicians all the time, but also to use my knowledge and interest in science. To be honest, I remember thinking, 'hmmm...maybe I'll go learn a bit about audio while I decide what to do with my life.' After only a few months, I knew I wanted to keep doing it. It was the perfect balance of science and music, and allowed me to work with musicians I admired."

Steve says that every day as a recording engineer is different. His main duties fall into three major categories: pre-production, recording, and post-production. A day at work could involve any combination of one or many of these tasks. In the following paragraphs, Steve details his specific responsibilities in each category:

Pre-Production. "As a recording engineer, it is important to plan properly for any recording session. The first thing to do is to gather all the information available about the project. I speak with the musicians and the producer about what music we will be recording, what instru-

ments we are recording, where we should do it, what equipment we need, whether or not we need to hire an assistant engineer, what the schedule will be, what transportation is needed, and how much everything will cost. After all of these details are worked out, I make a set of plans for the session, and usually try to listen to the music at a rehearsal or a concert sometime before the recording so I can learn the music better. I also need scores if it is classical music."

Recording. "The recording sessions for classical and jazz music are usually between three and five days long. In general, we record the songs over and over again until everyone is happy with the performances, and then we pick the best takes to put on the final CD. If it is classical music, we will set up all of our equipment in a church or a concert hall and record the musicians playing in there. We do this to capture the natural acoustics of the spaces where that music is usually performed. If it is a jazz recording session, we usually record in a recording studio where we have a little more control over the acoustics, and we can add any artificial reverberation or sound effects that are needed. Popular music recordings are also made in recording studios, and usually can last between a few days and a few weeks. In popular music recordings, the instruments are often recorded one at a time, whereas in classical and jazz recordings, the instruments are usually recorded at the same time."

Post-Production. "For classical recordings, most of the post-production consists of editing. During the recording session, the musicians played the music over and over until they played each part the best they could. In editing, we take all the best parts from the recording, and attach them together to make the finished song. For jazz and pop recordings, most of the editing is done during the recording session, so post-production involves mostly mixing and mastering. During the recording sessions, the sound from each microphone is recorded separately onto a single space or 'track.' If you have eight drum microphones, two piano microphones, two bass microphones, one guitar microphone, and one voice microphone, then you have 14 separate recorded sounds or tracks. In order to put this music onto a CD, all of those tracks have to be 'mixed down' to two tracks (left and right) so that people can play them on headphones or a regular stereo. This means adjusting how much of each original track gets put onto left or right and also if each of those sounds needs to be changed in some way. Then we use other equipment to process the sounds in order to make them the way we want."

DO I HAVE WHAT IT TAKES TO BE AN AUDIO RECORDING ENGINEER?

Being a recording engineer requires both technical skills and communication skills. "In the recording studio environment," says Ken Pohlmann, Director of Music Engineering at the University of Miami Frost School of Music, "engineering skills are clearly important, but personal skills are also very important. Music recording is an intensely personal effort and one

complicated by ego, jealousy, and loyalty. A successful recording engineer must be extremely knowledgeable and fast while working, able to keep current with new music and recording techniques, and also be able to handle difficult personal situations. Successful recording engineers must possess a uniquely aggressive and laidback personality that allows them to proactively market themselves and prove themselves as being best suited for a particular project."

Recording engineers must also continue to learn throughout their careers since recording technology changes constantly. "In the corporate world of music engineering," says Ken, "it is extremely important to develop high-level skills, and also keep those skills up-to-date. Technology moves quickly, and engineers are valued by their ability to keep up with the latest engineering knowledge and tools. Good engineers are essentially students for the life of their career, always learning new techniques and skills."

HOW DO I BECOME AN AUDIO RECORDING ENGINEER?
Education
High School

You should take music courses to learn an instrument, study voice, or learn composition. High school orchestras and bands are an excellent source for both practicing and studying music performance. You should also take classes in computer sciences, mathematics, business, and, if offered, electronics. A drama or broadcast journalism class may allow you access to a sound booth, and the opportunity to assist with audio engineering for live theatrical productions and radio programs.

Postsecondary Training

More than ever before, postsecondary training is an essential step for becoming a successful recording engineer. This is when you will make your first contacts and be introduced to many of the highly technical (and continually changing) aspects of the field. To learn about educational opportunities in the United States and abroad, visit the Web sites of the Audio Engineering Society (http://www.aes.org) or of *Mix Magazine* (http://mixonline.com).

Seminars and workshops offer the most basic level of education. This may be the best way to obtain an early, hands-on understanding of audio recording and prepare for entry-level apprentice positions. These programs are intended to introduce students to the equipment and technical aspects of the field, such as microphones, sound reinforcement, audio processing devices, tape and DAT machines, digital processing, and sound editing. Students will also become familiar with the newest technologies in the audio field, such as MIDI (musical instrument digital interface), synthesis, sampling, and current music software. A seminar can last from a couple of hours to several weeks. Many workshops are geared toward in-depth study of a certain aspect of recording such as mixing, editing, or music production.

Students looking for a more comprehensive course of study in specific areas of the recording industry can enroll in technical school or community college programs. Depending on the curriculum, these programs can take from several weeks to up to a year to complete. The most complete level of postsecondary education is a two- or four-year degree from a university. At many universities, students have access to state-of-the-art equipment and a teaching staff of knowledgeable professionals in the industry. Universities incorporate music, music technology, and music business in a comprehensive curriculum that prepare graduates to be highly competitive in the industry. "Many engineers opt for subsequent higher degree study," says Ken Pohlmann, "or perhaps pursue an MBA to advance to management positions."

Certification and Training

In the broadcast industry, engineers can be certified by the Society of Broadcast Engineers (http://www.sbe.org). Certification is recommended because this step shows your dedication to the field and your level of competence. After completing technical training and meeting strict qualifications, you can also join the society as a member or associate member. Membership gives you access to educational seminars, conferences, and a weekly job line.

Internships and Volunteerships

After high school, seek experience as an intern or apprentice, or begin postsecondary training in audio at a university or college or trade school. Because most professional recording studios and broadcasters prefer to offer apprenticeship positions to students who have some previous experience in audio, those who have completed some trade school courses may have better chances at landing jobs. Most university and college programs offer semester internship programs at professional recording studios as a way of earning credit. All students in Ken Pohlmann's Music Engineering Technology program at the University of Miami are strongly encouraged to pursue an internship, usually over the summer. "Internships," he explains, "give students a good opportunity to 'test drive' a career choice before committing to it after graduation. Similarly, an internship allows employers to evaluate a student as a potential employee; in many cases, an internship leads to a subsequent job offer following graduation. Internship positions range from an assistant in a recording studio to an audio software author in a corporation. Particularly at the undergraduate level, internships involve hands-on experiences. At the graduate level, students tend to work as applications engineers, often within teams."

Any experience you can get working in or around music will provide excellent background for this field. You can take up an instrument in the school band or orchestra, or perform with your own band. You might also have the opportunity to work behind the scenes with a music group, serving as a business manager, helping set up sound systems, or working as a technician in a school sound recording studio or radio station.

WHO WILL HIRE ME?

Though most major recording studios are located in metropolitan areas such as New York and Los Angeles, many cities across the country have vibrant music scenes. Talented, skilled engineers will always be in demand, no matter the size of the recording studio or the employment setting. "Career opportunities," says Ken Pohlmann, "are available in traditional audio companies, as well as in many major corporations that are relatively new to the field. For example, computer hardware and software companies and telephone service providers are tightly integrated into the music business and need skilled music engineers. On the other hand, low-cost home and project studios that can produce very good recordings challenge the traditional business model of large 'mothership' recording studios. Although many employment opportunities remain in the major studios, one must be very aware of alternative employment in smaller studios and stay flexible in the projects that they accept. Many recording engineers, for example, are self-employed, and must be able to quickly move from project to project."

Engineers also work for broadcast companies, engineering sound for radio and TV programs. Some recording engineers work for video production companies and corporate media libraries, helping to create in-house company presentations and films.

Most audio engineers begin their career in small studios as assistants, called *studio technicians*, and have varied

A World of Employment Options Available for Audio Engineering Graduates

The editors of *What Can I Do Now?: Music* asked Ken Pohlmann, Director of Music Engineering at the University of Miami Frost School of Music, to detail the job opportunities that are available to graduates of his program:

"Graduates of the Music Engineering Technology program receive jobs throughout the audio industry as recording engineers, audio systems engineers, multimedia authors, manufacturer's technical representatives, and audio designers, or accept positions in sound reinforcement companies, audio and video postproduction studios, studio acoustical design, and installation firms.

"Students seeking more artistic careers have taken positions with recording studios, working as mixing engineers, where their recording credits range from Vladimir Horowitz to the film score for *Batman*. Graduates have recorded and produced some of the best musicians in the business including Aaron Neville, Bee Gees, Chicago Symphony, Dallas Symphony, Everclear, Gloria Estefan, Incubus, Jeff Beck, Johnny Cash, Kyuss, L7, Los Lobos, Madonna, Michael Jackson, New Found Glory, New York Philharmonic, Prince, Rolling Stones, Sheryl Crowe, Stevie Wonder, Wallflowers, and many others.

"Other students working in motion picture sound have mixed the soundtracks for many outstanding motion pictures. For example, one graduate, Myron Nettinga, was awarded an Oscar for Best Sound for co-mixing the motion picture *Black Hawk Down*.

Some students work for studios or record labels including Cherokee Studios, Clinton Studios, Dorian Records, Doppler, Editel-Chicago, Howard Schwartz Studios, Hit Factory Criteria, Limelite Studios, Lionshare Studios, Miami Sound Machine, Middle Ear/Bee Gees, New River Studio, Norwegian Broadcasting Company, Pacific Ocean Post, Paisley Park, Sigma Sound, Sunset Sound, VTA, Yamaha R&D Studios, and many others.

"The Music Engineering program also places students in audio manufacturing companies. A partial listing of their employers reads like a 'who's who' of the audio industry: Alesis, Analog Devices, Apogee, Apple Computer, Ariel, BGW, CBS News, Cirrus Logic, Columbia University, Compaq Computer, Delphi, Denon America, Digidesign, Dolby Laboratories, Disney Productions, EFX Systems, Euphonix, Federal Bureau of Investigation, General Motors, George Massenburg Labs, Harman International, Harrison, Hewlett-Packard, Jaffe Acoustics, JBL, Klark-Teknik, Korg, Microsoft, Motorola, National Semiconductor, NBC Broadcasting, Neve, Norwegian Cruise Lines, Otari, Philips-DuPont Optical, Polk Audio, Radio Caracas, Real Networks, Record Plant, Roland, Shure, Sonic Foundry, Sony, Soundworks, Studer-Revox, Syracuse University, Texas Instruments, 3M, Universal Studios, and many more."

responsibilities, which may entail anything from running out to pick up dinner for the musicians during a recording session, to helping the recording engineer in the mixing process. Positions in radio will also provide a good stepping-stone to a career in audio recording. Entry-level positions may be easier to come by at studios that specialize in educational recording and radio advertisements than at music recording studios.

WHERE CAN I GO FROM HERE?

Career advancement will depend upon an engineer's interests as well as on his or her hard work and perseverance. They may advance to the higher paying, glamorous (yet high-pressure) position of music producer, either as an independent producer or working for a record label. Recording engineers may also advance to positions in the radio or television industries or in corporate settings, which usually offer better pay than studio work. If engineers wish to stay in the field of audio recording, they can advance to managerial positions or choose to open their own recording studio.

"In the future," says Steve Bellamy, "I would like to take a larger role in the promotion of jazz music and improvisational musicians. I am currently building a Web site that will help do this and also starting a small jazz festival. I started with my own business and am now enjoying working for a larger facility, but in the future, I think I would also like to go back to having my own studio. I like being able to decide which artists to work with and to collaborate more deeply with them. While I like technology, I am not so attached to it as I am to the music. Technology keeps changing and it is easy to learn new equipment and software as it comes out. The real challenge is making it all work towards a greater artistic goal. I think anyone considering this field should have a goal for themselves—something beyond learning a piece of gear or getting a job. The industry changes rapidly enough that there is no telling what opportunities will present themselves each year, but if you have a goal, you are better able to make wise choices along the way. My goal will continue to be to work with talented musicians who are doing new and creative things."

WHAT ARE THE SALARY RANGES?

Recent audio engineering graduates who are employed by corporations earn much higher starting salaries (approximately $60,000 annually, according to industry sources) than those employed by recording studios (approximately $20,000 a year).

According to the U.S. Department of Labor, the median income for sound engineering technicians was approximately $39,380 in 2004. At the low end of the scale, about 10 percent of these workers made less than $19,460. The highest paid 10 percent made $82,610 or more. Sound engineering technicians who are

Related Jobs

- broadcast engineers
- cable television technicians
- communications equipment technicians
- disc jockeys
- electronics engineering technicians
- music producers
- musicians

employed in the sound recording industry earned mean annual salaries of $44,130 in 2004, and those employed by software publishers earned $68,650. Audio engineers in the broadcast industry often earn higher salaries than those in the music industry. Generally, those working at television stations earned more than those working at radio stations.

Benefits packages will vary from business to business. Audio recording engineers employed by a recording company or by a broadcast station receive health insurance and paid vacation. Other benefits may include dental and eye care, life and disability insurance, and a pension plan.

WHAT IS THE JOB OUTLOOK?

Employment in this field is expected to grow about as fast as the average through 2014, according to the U.S. Department of Labor. "The audio industry is a growth industry," says Ken Pohlmann. "The proliferation of digital audio technology, combined with the Internet, has created unprecedented career opportunities. However, to take advantage of these opportunities, students must be well prepared with rigorous knowledge of mathematics, science, audio engineering, electrical engineering, and computer programming skills. In particular, there is no question that the audio business is computer-based, in terms of its production, dissemination, and reception by consumers. Anyone seeking a career in the audio field must gather as much technological skill and artistic knowledge as possible to compete in this exciting field."

Music Conductors and Directors

SUMMARY

Definition
Music conductors direct large groups of musicians or singers in the performance of a piece of music. They sometimes carry the title of music director, which implies a wider area of responsibilities, including administrative and managerial duties.

Alternative Job Titles
None

Salary Range
$15,000 to $40,000 to $500,000+

Educational Requirements
High school diploma

Certification or Licensing
None available

Employment Outlook
About as fast as the average

High School Subjects
Music
Theater

Personal Interests
Entertaining/performing
Music

"The most interesting thing that has happened to me in the field of music is the realization of how important music is in everyone's life, but especially mine," says Dr. Bruce Chamberlain, a college educator and director of the Tucson Symphony Orchestra's Chorus. "I have seen folks become overwhelmed by the beauty and majesty of Beethoven's Ninth Symphony, and completely enthralled by the intimacy and profundity of a Josquin motet. Being able to bring these concepts and sounds alive with people at various stages of musical development is a constant source of amazement and satisfaction for me. I simply cannot imagine an entire day without music. Music literally sought and captured me for a career—not the other way around."

WHAT DOES A MUSIC CONDUCTOR AND DIRECTOR DO?

Conducting, whether it be of a symphony orchestra, an opera, a chorus, a theater pit orchestra, a marching band, or even a big swing band, is an enormously complex and demanding occupation to which only the exceptional individual can possibly aspire, with hope of even moderate success. *Music conductors* must have multiple skills and talents. First and foremost, they must be consummate musicians.

Not only should they have mastered an instrument, but they also must know music and be able to interpret the score of any composition. They should have an unerring ear and a bearing that commands the respect of the musicians. Conductors need to be sensitive to the musicians, sympathetic to their problems, and able to inspire them to bring out the very best they have to offer. Conductors must also have a sense of showmanship. Some conductors have advanced farther than others because their dramatic conducting style helps bring in larger audiences and greater receipts. The conductor must also be a psychologist who can deal with the multiplicity of complex and temperamental personalities presented by a large ensemble of musicians and singers. Conductors must exude personal charm; orchestras are always fund-raising, and the conductor is frequently expected to meet major donors to keep their goodwill. Finally, and in line with fund-raising, music conductors and directors are expected to have administrative skills and to understand the business and financial problems that face the orchestra organization.

Conductors are distinguished by their baton technique and arm and body movements. These can vary widely from conductor to conductor, some being reserved and holding to minimal movements, others using sweeping baton strokes and broad arm and body gestures. There is no right or wrong way to conduct; it is a highly individualized art, and great conductors produce excellent results using extremely contrasting styles. The conductor's fundamental purpose in leading, regardless of style, is to set the tempo and rhythm of a piece. Conductors must be sure that the orchestra is following their interpretation of the music, and they must resolve any problems that the score poses. Failure to render a composition in a way that is pleasing to the public and the critics is usually blamed on the conductor, although there is a school that feels that both the conductor and the musicians are to blame, or that at least it is difficult to tell which one is most at fault.

The quality of a performance is probably most directly related to the conductor's rehearsal techniques. It is during rehearsals that conductors must diagnose and correct to their satisfaction the musical, interpretive, rhythmic, balance, and intonation problems encountered by the orchestra. They must work with each unit of the orchestra individually and the entire ensemble as a whole; this may include soloist instrumentalists and singers as well as a chorus. Some conductors rehearse every detail of a score while others have been known to emphasize only certain parts during rehearsal. Some are quiet and restrained at rehearsals, while others work to a feverish emotional pitch. The sound that an orchestra makes is also identified with the conductor, and for some, such as Eugene Ormandy, formerly of the Philadelphia Orchestra, the tone of an orchestra becomes a recognizable signature. Tone is determined by the conductor's use of the various sections of the orchestra. The brass section, for instance, can be instructed to play so that the sound is bright, sharp, and piercing, or they can play to produce a rich, sonorous, and heavy sound. The strings can play the vibrato broadly to produce a thick, lush tone or play with little vibrato to produce a thinner, more delicate sound.

The working conditions of conductors and directors range as widely as their earnings. The conductors of small musical groups at the community level may rehearse in a member's basement, a community center, a high school gym, or in a church or temple. Performances may be held in some of those same places. Lighting, heating or cooling, sound equipment, and musical instrument quality may all be less than adequate. On the other hand,

conductors of major orchestras in the larger metropolitan centers usually have ideal working conditions, generally having the same outstanding facilities for rehearsal and performance. Many universities, colleges, and conservatories, even some of the smaller ones, also have state-of-the-art facilities.

WHAT IS IT LIKE TO BE A MUSIC CONDUCTOR OR DIRECTOR?

Dr. Bruce Chamberlain has been a choral conductor in higher education for 30 years. He is currently a professor of music and director of choral activities at the University of Arizona in Tucson, Arizona, where he leads a choral studies program with 25 graduate majors, eight choirs, and more than 500 singers. Three years ago, he was asked by the Tucson Symphony Orchestra (TSO) to organize and direct its newly founded TSO Chorus. Subsequently, he has prepared more than 12 concerts for the TSO and conducted several concerts for them. In addition, he is the director of choirs at Trinity Presbyterian Church in Tucson, the oldest and largest Presbyterian church in the area.

"I was always attracted to music—from age 10 when I first started taking piano lessons," says Bruce. "I originally went to college as a pianist to become the next Van Cliburn. It was as a freshman in college that I sang with Eugene Ormandy and the Philadelphia Orchestra, and the Mendelssohn Club of Philadelphia, that I got bitten with the choral bug and have been hooked ever since."

Mean Annual Earnings for Music Conductors and Directors by Employer, 2004

Employer	Mean Annual Earnings
Motion picture and video industries	$75,720
Sound recording industries	$50,860
Performing arts companies	$46,360
Colleges and universities	$44,560
Religious organizations	$41,900
Elementary and secondary schools	$40,520

Source: U.S. Department of Labor

To Be a Successful Music Conductor And Director, You Should . . .

- have self-discipline and integrity
- have a love of music
- have self-confidence in your ability to lead and interpret music
- be a strong leader
- have strong organization skills

"In my present position I only teach, conduct, and work with graduate students. In the past, however, I have taught liberal arts interdisciplinary courses, both semesters of undergraduate conducting, choral literature, and other courses. At the University of Arizona, however, I conduct one ensemble, The Arizona Choir (a 40-voice, all graduate student choir), teach graduate level conducting, teach a choral seminar (a four-semester sequence of literature and techniques for graduate choral conducting majors), and I direct the lecture recital and dissertation projects for the doctor of musical arts candidates."

DO I HAVE WHAT IT TAKES TO BE A MUSIC CONDUCTOR OR DIRECTOR?

Conductors require a high degree of self-discipline and unquestioned integrity in order to fill a difficult and complex lead-ership role. It is also important that they learn all the aspects of the business and social functions of an orchestra. Like musicians and composers, conductors must have talent, a quality that cannot be taught or acquired. They must have supreme self-confidence in their ability to lead and interpret the music of the great masters. They must convince both audience and ensemble that they are in command.

Bruce believes that the most important personal qualities for musical conductors and directors are leadership, compassion, integrity, the ability and willingness to mentor, as well as "good ears."

HOW DO I BECOME A MUSIC CONDUCTOR OR DIRECTOR?

Education

High School

Formal training in at least one musical instrument is necessary for a future as a music conductor or director. Keyboard instruction is particularly important. In high school, participation in a concert band, jazz ensemble, choir, or orchestra will teach you about group performing and how the various parts contribute to a whole sound. Some high schools may offer opportunities to conduct school music groups.

Postsecondary Training

It is unlikely that many people start out at a very early point in life with the goal of becoming a music conductor. Most conductors begin studying music at an early age and possibly, at some later, more mature point in life, may discover or suspect that they have the qualities to become a conductor. Some conductors become involved at the high school or college level, leading a small group for whom they may also do the arranging and possibly some composing. There are some courses specifically in conducting at advanced institutions, and interested students may take courses in composition, arranging, and orchestrating, which provide a good background for conducting. Some opportunities to conduct may arise in the university, and you may be able to study with a faculty member who conducts the school orchestra. Conductor training programs and apprenticeship programs, which are announced in the music trade papers, are also available.

It was once commonly thought that conducting was unteachable. That attitude has been changing, however, and some institutions have developed formalized programs to teach the art of conducting. The Paris Conservatory is particularly noted for its conducting instruction, and completion of that institution's course is said to pave the way to opportunities in conducting. The Julliard School is another institution known for its studies in conducting.

Conductors must acquire a multiplicity of skills in order to practice their art. These skills may be divided into three parts: technical, performance, and conducting.

Technical skills deal with the conductors' ability to control orchestral intonation, balance, and color; they must be advanced at sight-reading and transposi-tion in order to cope with orchestral scores. Conductors must acquire a comprehensive knowledge of all orchestral instruments and must themselves have mastery of at least one instrument, the piano probably being the most helpful. They must acquire skills in composition and music analysis, which presumes accomplished skills in counterpoint, harmony, musical structures, and orchestration. Finally, conductors must understand and be able to adapt musical styling.

Performance skills refer to conductors' own instrumental ability. Mastery of one instrument is important, but the more instruments conductors know, the better they will be able to relate to members of the orchestra. It is through knowledge of instruments that conductors develop their interpretive abilities.

Conducting skills involve the ability to use the baton and to control the timing, rhythm, and structure of a musical piece. Conductors must develop these skills at performances and at rehearsals. At rehearsals they must use their power and their intellect to blend the various elements of the orchestra and the composition into a single unified presentation. Conductors must also learn to use their whole bodies, along with the baton, to control the music.

Conductors require not only an extensive knowledge of music but also a strong general background in the arts and humanities. They should have a comprehensive knowledge of musical history as it fits into the general fabric of civilization along with competence in various languages, including French, German, Italian, and Latin. Language skills are particularly helpful in coaching singers. Familiarity with the history of Western civilization, particularly its literature, drama, and art, will also be valuable in the composer's musical frame of reference.

Internships and Volunteerships

You will have the opportunity to participate in an internship as a music student. You might teach music at a local high school, work for a local arts organization, or perhaps get the chance to work for a local symphony or music group. Internships, which often provide college credit, offer you the opportunity to learn about the field from conductors, directors, and other music professionals.

The best way to become familiar with the art of conducting is to study music and the great conductors themselves. It is not possible to understand conducting beyond the most superficial level without a good background in music. Students of conducting should go to as many musical presentations as they can, such as symphonies, operas, musical theater, and the like, and study the conductors, noting their baton techniques and their arm and body movements. Try to determine how the orchestra and audience respond to the gesturing of the conductors. There are also many associations, reference books, and biographies that provide detailed information about conductors and their art. One of the most prominent organizations is the American Symphony Orchestra League located in Washington, D.C. It holds a national

conference and conducting workshops each year.

WHO WILL HIRE ME?

There are many situations in which music conductors and directors may work. Music teachers in schools often take on conducting as a natural extension of their duties. Conservatories and institutions of higher learning frequently have fine orchestras, choruses, and bands that often choose conductors from the faculty. There are numerous summer festivals that employ conductors, and conductors may also find positions with community orchestras and choruses, local opera companies, and musical theater groups; even amateur groups sometimes hire outside conductors. For the very exceptional, of course, there is the possibility of conducting with famous orchestras, theaters, and opera companies, as well as the musical groups associated with broadcasting and film studios. Well-known conductors are in demand and travel a great deal, appearing as guest conductors with other orchestras or making personal appearances.

A career in conducting begins with a sound musical education. Working as an instrumentalist in an orchestral group, under a good conductor whose technique can be studied, is an important step toward conducting. The piano is an important instrument for conductors to know, because it will not only enable them to score and arrange more easily, it also will be useful in coaching singers, which many conductors do as a sideline, and in rehearsing an orchestra as an assistant conductor. That is not to say, however, that other instrumentalists do not also acquire a good background for conducting.

With a solid foundation in musical education and some experience with an orchestra, young conductors should seek any way possible to acquire experience conducting. There are many grants and fellowships you can apply for, and many summer music festivals advertise for conductors. These situations often present the opportunity to work or study under a famous conductor who has been engaged to oversee or administer a festival. Such experience is invaluable because it provides opportunities to make contacts for various other conducting positions. These may include apprenticeships, jobs with university choirs and orchestras (which may include a faculty position), or opportunities with community orchestras, small opera companies, or amateur groups that seek a professional music director. Experience in these positions can lead to offers with major orchestras, operas, or musical theater companies as an assistant or associate conductor.

Not everyone will want or be able to move into a major role as a conductor of a well-known orchestra. Many, in fact most, will remain in other positions such as those described. Those seeking to further their career as a conductor may want to invest in a personal manager who will find bookings and situations for ambitious young talent. More than likely, entering the conducting field will take more of an investment than most other careers. Music education, applying for grants and fellowships, and attending workshops, summer music camps, and festivals can add up to a considerable expense. Moving into a good conducting job may take time as well, and young people going into the field should not expect to reach the pinnacle of their profession until they are well into their 30s or 40s or even older.

WHERE CAN I GO FROM HERE?

There is no real hierarchy in an orchestra organization that one can climb to the role of conductor. The most likely advancement within an organization would be from the position of assistant or associate conductor or from that of the head first violinist, that is, the concertmaster. Conductors generally move from smaller conducting jobs to larger ones. A likely advancement would be from a small community orchestra or youth orchestra (probably a part-time position), to a small city orchestra (full- or part-time), and from there to a larger city orchestra, a mid-sized opera company, or directorship of a middle-level television or film company. Such advancement presumes that the conductor has had sufficient recognition and quality reviews to come to the attention of the larger musical groups.

Conductors who take the leadership of mid-sized city orchestras and opera companies may be in the hands of an agent or manager, who takes care of financial matters, guest bookings, and personal appearances. The agent will also be looking for advancement to more prestigious conducting jobs in the larger cities. At the point that conductors receive national or international recognition, it becomes a question of which major position they will accept as openings occur. It is unlikely that a major city orchestra would promote someone within the organization when the conductorship is open. It is more probable that a search committee will conduct an international search to find a big name conductor for the post. Conductors themselves can advance to top-level administrative positions, such as artistic director or executive director.

"In 10 years, which will be my 40th year [as a choral conductor in higher education]," says Bruce, "I plan to retire. I am presently in my career goal position (employed at a major, level-1 research university with a large choral program with multiple choirs, faculty, and graduate students). I do also enjoy my outlet with the professional symphony orchestra."

WHAT ARE THE SALARY RANGES?

The range of earnings for music conductors and directors is enormous, and there is variation from one category of conductors to another. For instance, many conductors work only part time and make quite small yearly incomes for their conducting endeavors. Part-time choir directors for churches and temples, for instance, make from $3,500 to $25,000 per year, while full-time directors make from $15,000 to $40,000 per year. Con-

> ### Related Jobs
>
> - arrangers
> - composers
> - directors of music associations
> - music producers
> - music teachers
> - musicians
> - singers

ductors of dance bands make from $300 to $1,200 per week. Opera and choral group conductors make as little as $8,000 per year working part time at the community level, but salaries range to over $100,000 per year for those with permanent positions with established companies in major cities. The same applies to symphony orchestra conductors who, for instance, make $25,000 to $40,000 per year conducting smaller, regional orchestras, but who can make $500,000 or more a year if they become the resident conductor of an internationally famous orchestra.

WHAT IS THE JOB OUTLOOK?

The operating cost for an orchestra continues to grow every year, and music organizations are in constant budget-trimming modes as have been most other professional business organizations in the last decade. This has tended to affect growth in the orchestra field and, accordingly, the number of conducting jobs. Additionally, the overall number of orchestras in the United States has grown only slightly in the last two decades. The number of orchestras in academia declined slightly while community, youth, and city orchestras for the most part increased slightly in number. The slight growth pattern of orchestra groups will not nearly accommodate the number of people who graduated from music school during that period and are trying to become conductors. The competition for music conductor and director jobs, already tight, will become even tighter in the next decade. Only the most talented people moving into the field will be able to find full-time jobs.

Musicians

SUMMARY

Definition
Musicians perform, compose, conduct, arrange, and teach music. Performing musicians may work alone or as part of a group or ensemble. They may play before live audiences in clubs or auditoriums, or they may perform on television or radio, in motion pictures, or in a recording studio.

Alternative Job Titles
Musical performers
Performing artist

Salary Range
$0 to $37,253 to $1,000,000+

Educational Requirements
High school diploma

Certification or Licensing
Required for certain positions

Employment Outlook
About as fast as the average

High School Subjects
English (writing/literature)
Music
Theater

Personal Interests
Entertaining/performing
Music
Theater

Jacquelyn Sellers, a professional musician for more than 30 years, says that the most incredible experience she has ever had as a musician was playing a composition she wrote for five horns with her colleagues from the Tucson Symphony Orchestra on the Great Wall in China. "In 1999, I composed a piece entitled 'Desert Suite for Five Horns,'" she recalls. "It was awarded second place in the International Horn Society's (IHS) Composition Competition, and we were invited to perform the piece at the IHS Horn Symposium held in Beijing, China, in July of 2000. We performed at a concert with over 3,000 people in attendance, and they had us come back for two encores! After the con-cert, we signed autographs for Chinese horn students, and it was such a blast. Two days later, we went to the Great Wall and brought our horns and music and played my piece. I still get choked up just thinking about what an awesome experience that was!"

WHAT DOES A MUSICIAN DO?

Instrumental musicians play one or more musical instruments, typically in a group and in some cases as featured soloists. Musical instruments are usually classified in several distinct categories according to the method by which they produce sound:

strings (violins, cellos, basses, etc.), which make sounds by vibrations from bowing or plucking; woodwinds (oboes, clarinets, saxophones), which make sounds by air vibrations through reeds; brass (trumpets, French horns, trombones, etc.), which make sounds by air vibrations through metal; and percussion (drums, pianos, triangles), which produce sounds by striking. Instruments can also be classified as electric or acoustic, especially in popular music. Synthesizers are another common instrument, and computer and other electronic technology increasingly is used for creating music.

Like other instrumental musicians, *singers* use their own voices as instruments to convey music. They aim to express emotion through lyric phrasing and characterization.

Musicians may play in symphony orchestras, dance bands, jazz bands, rock bands, country bands, or other groups or they might go it alone. Some musicians may play in recording studios either with their group or as a session player for a particular recording. Recordings are in the form of records, tapes, compact discs, videotape cassettes, and digital video discs. *Classical musicians* perform in concerts, opera performances, and chamber music concerts, and they may also play in theater orchestras, although theater music is not normally classical. The most talented ones may work as soloists with orchestras or alone in recitals. Some classical musicians accompany singers and choirs, and they may also perform in churches, temples, and other religious settings.

Musicians who play popular music make heavy use of such rhythm instruments as piano, bass, drums, and guitar. *Jazz musicians* also use woodwind and brass instruments, especially the saxophone and trumpet, and they extensively utilize the bass. Synthesizers are also commonly used as jazz instruments; some music is performed entirely on synthesizers, which can be programmed to imitate a variety of instruments and sounds. Musicians in jazz, blues, country, and rock groups play clubs, festivals, and concert halls and may perform music for recordings, television, and motion picture sound tracks. Occasionally, they themselves appear in a movie themselves. Other musicians compose, record, and perform entirely with electronic instruments, such as synthesizers and other devices. In the late 1970s, *rap artists* began using turntables as musical instruments, and later, samplers, which record a snippet of other songs and sounds, as part of their music.

Instrumental musicians and singers use their skills to convey the form and meaning of written music. They work to achieve precision, fluency, and emotion within a piece of music, whether through an instrument or through their own voice. Musicians practice constantly to perfect their techniques.

Many musicians supplement their incomes through teaching, while others teach full time, taking paying gigs occasionally. *Voice and instrumental music teachers* work in colleges, high schools, elementary schools, conservatories, and in their own studios; often they give concerts and recitals featuring their students. Many professional musicians give private lessons. Students learn to read music, develop their voices, breathe correctly, and hold their instruments properly.

Choral directors lead groups of singers in schools and other organizations. Church choirs, community oratorio societies, and professional symphony choruses are among the groups that employ choral directors outside of school settings. Choral directors audition singers, select music, and direct singers in achieving the tone, variety, intensity, and phrasing that they feel is required. *Orchestra conductors* do the same with instrumental musicians. Many work in schools and smaller communities, but the best conduct large orchestras in major cities. Some are resident instructors, while others travel constantly, making guest appearances with major national and foreign orchestras. They are responsible for the overall sound and quality of their orchestras.

Individuals also write and prepare music for themselves or other musicians to play and sing. *Composers* write the original music for symphonies, songs, or operas using musical notation to express their ideas through melody, rhythm, and harmony. *Arrangers* and *orchestrators* take a composer's work and transcribe it for the various orchestra sections or individual instrumentalists and singers to perform; they prepare music for film scores, musical theater, television, or recordings. *Copyists* assist composers and arrangers by copying down the various parts of a composition, each of which

Advice for Aspiring Musicians

Jacquelyn Sellers, principal horn player of the Tucson Symphony Orchestra (TSO), offers the following advice to young horn players:

- Find yourself the best private instructor you can. It's so important to meet with a professional musician every week who can guide you and give constructive criticism.

- Play in as many groups as you can—bands, orchestras, small chamber groups, jazz ensembles.

- Don't let anyone tell you that you can't play jazz as a horn player.

- Listen to live music as much as possible. We have a program here in Tucson where the students who are in the youth orchestra can attend TSO concerts for free. It is so important to hear live professionals doing what you want to do in the future.

is played by a different section of the orchestra. *Librettists* write words to opera and musical theater scores, and *lyricists* write words to songs and other short musical pieces. A number of songwriters compose both music and lyrics, and many are musicians who perform their own songs.

Work conditions for musicians vary greatly. Performing musicians generally work in the evenings and on weekends. They also spend much time practicing and rehearsing for performances. Their workplace can be almost anywhere, from a swanky club to a high school gymnasium to a dark, dingy bar. Many concerts are given outdoors and in a variety of weather conditions. Performers may be given a star's dressing room, share a mirror in a church basement, or have to change in a bar's storeroom. They may work under the hot camera lights of film or television sets or tour with a troupe in subzero temperatures. They may work amid the noise and confusion of a large rehearsal of a Broadway show or in the relative peace and quiet of a small recording studio. Seldom are two days in a performer's life exactly alike.

Many musicians and singers travel a great deal. More prominent musicians may travel with staffs who make their arrangements and take care of wardrobes and equipment. Their accommodations are usually quite comfortable, if not luxurious, and they generally play in major urban centers. Lesser-known musicians may have to take care of all their own arrangements and put up with modest accommodations in relatively remote places. Some musicians perform on the streets, at subway or bus stations, and other places likely to have a great deal of passersby. Symphony orchestra musicians probably travel less than most, but musicians in major orchestras usually travel first-class.

The chief characteristic of musical employment is its lack of continuity. Few musicians work full time, and most experience periods of unemployment between engagements. Most work day jobs to supplement their music or performing incomes. Those who are in great demand generally have agents and managers to help direct their careers.

Music teachers affiliated with institutions work the same hours as other classroom teachers. Many of these teachers, however, spend time after school and on weekends directing and instructing school vocal and instrumental groups. Teachers may also have varied working conditions. They may teach in a large urban school, conducting five different choruses each day, or they may work in several rural elementary schools and spend much time driving from school to school.

College or university instructors may divide their time between group and individual instruction. They may teach several musical subjects and may be involved with planning and producing school musical events. They may also supervise student music teachers when they do their practice teaching.

Private music teachers work part time or full time out of their own homes or in separate studios. The ambiance of their workplace is in accordance with the size and nature of their clientele.

WHAT IS IT LIKE TO BE A MUSICIAN?

Jacquelyn Sellers is the principal horn player for the Tucson Symphony Orchestra (TSO). She has performed with the orchestra since 1982. "I come from a musical family," she says. "My mother was a vocal and piano teacher, my aunt and uncle both played in the Phoenix Symphony Orchestra, and my grandfather was a choral director. With all that music in the house, it was fairly natural to choose music as a career. I couldn't imagine doing anything else."

Jacquelyn says that her day always begins with a cup of coffee and her mouthpiece. "I buzz for 20 to 30 minutes on my mouthpiece as the first part of my warm-up," she explains. "I then go through a series of arpeggios and scales (you NEVER stop practicing them!) and other exercises that get me ready to play for the day.

"One of the things I like best about being a symphony musician is that every day is different. Some weeks, my rehearsals will be only orchestral and in the evenings. Some weeks, I'll be playing with the Wind Quintet during the day at various elementary schools, as part of our 'Music in the Schools' program. But typically, after my warm-up, I'll do chores around the house, take our little dog, Sophie, for a walk and do some kind of exercise for myself. Then I do what I call my 'second set.' These are more exercises of scales and other etudes that I play for about 30 minutes. Then I'll practice whatever music is looming at the present moment. Sometimes it is a Mahler symphony, other times it is a Mozart piano concerto and a Strauss tone poem."

In the afternoons, Jacquelyn teaches private horn lessons. "I have 12 students that range in age from 10 to 41," she says. "I love teaching."

In the evening, Jacquelyn usually participates in TSO rehearsals from 7:00 P.M. to 9:30 P.M. "If we don't have rehearsal," she says, "then I will do one more practice session for upcoming concerts so that I am always prepared for the next concert."

To Be a Successful Musician, You Should . . .

- have musical talent and ability
- hold yourself to high ethical and musical standards
- be punctual for practices and performances
- be dedicated and willing to work hard to reach your goals
- be willing to practice for long hours
- be willing to accept constructive criticism regarding your abilities

DO I HAVE WHAT IT TAKES TO BE A MUSICIAN?

Jacquelyn believes that musicians must hold themselves to high ethical and high musical standards. "I try to teach my students that in addition to being a fabulous musician you must also be a fabulous human being," she says. "This means that you don't put other people down and that you never speak ill of others, especially behind their backs. Have something nice to say to everyone and be encouraging to someone who might be having a rough time. Additionally, always have your music prepared and arrive early to every rehearsal and concert."

Hard work and dedication are key factors in a musical career, but music is an art form, and like those who practice any of the fine arts, musicians will succeed according to the amount of musical talent they have. Those who have talent and are willing to make sacrifices to develop it are the ones most likely to succeed. How much talent and ability one has is always open to speculation and opinion, and it may take years of studying and practice before musicians can assess their own degrees of limitation.

There are other requirements necessary to becoming a professional musician that are just as important as training, education, and study. Foremost among these is a love of music that is strong enough to endure the arduous training and working life of a musician. To become an accomplished musician and to be recognized in the field requires an uncommon degree of dedication, self-discipline, and drive. Musicians who would move ahead must practice constantly, with a determination to improve their technique and quality of performance. Musicians also need to develop an emotional toughness that will help them deal with rejection, indifference to their work, and ridicule from critics, which will be especially prevalent early in their careers. There is also praise and adulation along the way, which is easier to take but also requires a certain psychological handling.

For musicians interested in careers in popular music, little to no formal training is necessary. Many popular musicians teach themselves to play their instruments, which often results in the creation of new and exciting playing styles. Quite often, popular musicians do not even know how to read music. Some would say that many rock musicians do not even know how to play their instruments. This was especially true in the early days of the punk era (circa late 1970s/early 1980s). Most musicians, however, have a natural talent for rhythm and melody.

Many musicians often go through years of paying their dues—that is, receiving little money, respect, or attention for their efforts. Therefore, they must have a strong sense of commitment to their careers and to their creative ideas.

HOW DO I BECOME A MUSICIAN?
Education

Jacquelyn started playing horn at the age of 12. "I had a private teacher," she says, "and this is probably the most important thing a young student can do to prepare for a career in music." In college, Jacquelyn majored in horn performance at Arizona State University (ASU). After graduating from ASU, she pursued a master's degree at Indiana University and studied with Philip Farkas. "He was the greatest horn pedagogue in the world and is still considered one of the greatest teachers on the horn ever," she recalls. "I was lucky enough that, three weeks after graduating from Indiana University, with my master of music degree, I won the audition for principal horn of the Tucson Symphony, and I've been here ever since."

High School

If you are interested in becoming a musician, you will probably have begun to develop your musical skills long before you entered high school. While you are in high school, however, there are a number of classes you can take that will help you broaden your knowledge. Naturally, take band, orchestra, or choir classes, depending on your interest. In addition, you should also take mathematics classes, since any musician needs to understand counting, rhythms, and beats. Many professional musicians write at least some of their own music, and a strong math background is very helpful for this. If your high school offers courses in music history or appreciation, be sure to take these. Finally, take classes that will improve your communication skills and your understanding of people and emotions, such as English and psychology. If you are interested in working in the classical music field, you will most likely need a college degree to succeed in this area. Therefore, be sure to round out your high school education by taking other college preparatory classes. Finally, no matter what type of musician you want to be, you will need to devote much of your after-school time to your private study and practice of music.

Postsecondary Training

Depending on your interest, especially if it is popular music, further formal education is not required. College or conservatory degrees are only required for those who plan to teach in academic institutions. Nevertheless, you will only benefit from continued education.

Scores of colleges and universities have excellent music schools, and there are numerous conservatories that offer degrees in music. Many schools have noted musicians on their staff, and music students often have the advantage of studying under a professor who has a distinguished career in music. By studying with someone like this, you will not only learn more about music and performance, but you will also begin to make valuable connections in the field. You should know that having talent and a high grade point average do not always ensure entry into the top music schools. Competition for positions is extremely tough. You will probably have to audition, and only the most talented are accepted.

College undergraduates in music school generally take courses in music theory, harmony, counterpoint, rhythm, melody, ear training, applied music, and music history. Courses in composing, arranging, and conducting are available in most comprehensive music schools. Students will also have to take courses such as English and psychology, along with a regular academic program.

Certification and Training

Musicians who want to teach in state elementary and high schools must be state certified. To obtain a state certificate, musicians must satisfactorily complete a degree-granting course in music education at an institution of higher learning. About 600 institutions in the United States offer programs in music education that qualify students for state certificates. Music education programs include many of the same courses mentioned earlier for musicians in general. They also include education courses and supervised practice teaching. Teaching in colleges and universities or in conservatories generally requires a graduate degree in music. Widely recognized musicians, however, sometimes receive positions in higher education without having obtained a degree.

The American Guild of Organists offers a number of voluntary, professional certifications to its members. Visit the guild's Web site (http://www.agohq.org) for more information.

Internships and Volunteerships

Aspiring musicians do not generally participate in internships in the same manner as students in other fields. Instead, they immerse themselves in the study and performance of music at an early age in order to improve their knowledge of musical styles and techniques and hone their talents. If they attend college, they continue performing music, honing their talents, and learning about the field. College music students who are interested in becoming educators work as student teachers to gain experience and receive feedback regarding their teaching abilities

The first step to exploring your interest in a musical career is to become involved with music. Elementary schools, high schools, and institutions of higher education all present a number of options for musical training and performance, including choirs, ensembles, bands, and orchestras. You may also have chances to perform in school musicals and talent shows. Those involved with services at churches, synagogues, or other religious institutions have excellent opportunities for exploring their

interest in music. If you can afford to, take private music lessons.

Besides learning more about music, you will most likely have the chance to play in recitals arranged by your teacher. You may also want to attend special summer camps or programs that focus on the field. Interlochen Center for the Arts (http://www.interlochen.org), for example, offers summer camps for students from the elementary to the high school level. College, university, and conservatory students gain valuable performance experience by appearing in recitals and playing in bands, orchestras, and school shows. The more enterprising students in high school and in college form their own bands and begin earning money by playing while still in school.

It is important for you to take advantage of every opportunity to audition so that you become comfortable with this process. There are numerous community amateur and semiprofessional theater groups throughout the United States that produce musical plays and operettas in which beginning musicians can gain playing experience.

If you have made recordings of your music, you might want to create a profile on MySpace.com, which will allow you to share your music with millions of people around the world.

Labor Unions

Professional musicians generally hold membership in the American Federation of Musicians (AFL-CIO), and concert soloists also hold membership in the American Guild of Musical Artists

Interview: Diane Christiansen

Diane Christiansen is a member of the band Dolly Varden, which according to its Web site, "features intelligent, textured songwriting, soaring harmony vocals, and a soulful, melodic mix of rock, country and pop influences." The band has released four critically acclaimed albums. In addition to her work in Dolly Varden, Diane is also an accomplished artist. She discussed her musical and artistic careers with the editors of *What Can I Do Now?: Music*.

Q. Tell us about your career as a musician.

A. I have been in a band called Dolly Varden for about 10 years. I studied classical music at a boarding high school called Interlochen Arts Academy in Michigan and then gave up performing until I met my best friend, Steve Dawson, in 1986. We formed a band called Stump the Host, which was very raw and twangy, and later formed Dolly Varden. [Visit http://www.dollyvarden.com to learn more about Dolly Varden and to hear samples of its music.]

Q. What are the best and worst parts of being a musician?

A. The best part of playing/touring is the incredible connective tissue formed between people creating music and between them and their audiences. It is a spiritual high I have never experienced in other aspects of life.

The worst part is how really hard being poor, and being treated poorly, is on a person. Being a traveling musician not supported by a major label with deep pockets is truly rough. It is made worthwhile only by the love of playing. I was told at a young age only to go into the arts if you couldn't stop yourself, because IT IS ROUGH. The upshot is that never has our consumer-driven society more needed soul and spiritual connection; so if you can hack the complete lack of cultural support for the arts, go for it.

Q. Why did you decide to become an artist?

A. I started identifying myself as an artist at nine years old when I lived in France with my family. I had a hellish year, and making images and toys out of cloth with hand-drawn faces became a refuge for me.

Q. What type of formal training in art have you had?

A. My formal "training" started late in college when I took a drawing class and felt like I had fallen into the loving arms of meaning and purpose. I went to graduate school at the Art Institute of Chicago several years after that.

Q. What are the most important aspects of a great work of art?

A. I can't define great art, but I know that I personally am sparked by stuff that resonates both personally and in a huge collective way. Frequently, really simple things, such as a neighborhood graffiti artist's repeated images painted on buildings or one of my eight-year-old nephew's draw-

(continued on next page)

(continued from previous page)

ings, come back to me over and over and punctuate my days in a way that makes life worth living. I can only hope to provide that flint for someone else's life.

Q. What advice would you give to high school students who are interested in pursuing artistic careers?

A. For young people interested in the arts I would encourage them to release the super-seductive idea of being successful and ask, if that were subtracted, what would draw them to creating? Whatever is leftover when that ego stuff is out of the way, that's the entire purpose right there.

(AFL-CIO). Singers can belong to a branch of Associated Actors and Artists of America (AFL-CIO). Music teachers in schools often hold membership in MENC: The National Association for Music Education (formerly Music Educators National Conference).

WHO WILL HIRE ME?

Musicians, singers, and related workers hold approximately 249,000 jobs in the United States. Most musicians work in large urban areas and are particularly drawn to the major recording centers, such as Chicago, New York City, Los Angeles, Nashville, and Miami Beach. Most musicians find work in churches, temples, schools, clubs, restaurants, and cruise lines, at weddings, in opera and ballet productions, and on film, television, and radio. Religious organizations are the largest single source of work for musicians.

Full-time positions as a musician in a choir, symphony orchestra, or band are few and are held only by the most tal-

ented. Musicians who are versatile and willing to work hard will find a variety of opportunities available, but all musicians should understand that work is not likely to be steady or provide much security. Many musicians support themselves in another line of work while pursuing their musical careers on a part-time basis. Busy musicians often hire agents to find employers and negotiate contracts or conditions of employment.

WHERE CAN I GO FROM HERE?

Popular musicians, once they have become established with a band, advance by moving up to more famous bands or by taking leadership of their own group. Bands may advance from playing small clubs to larger halls and even stadiums and festivals. They may receive a recording contract; if their songs or recordings prove successful, they can command higher fees for their contracts. Symphony orchestra musicians advance by moving to the head of their section of the orchestra. They can also move up to a position such as assistant or associate conductor. Once instrumental musicians acquire a reputation as accomplished artists, they receive engagements that are of higher status and remuneration, and they may come into demand as soloists. As their reputations develop, both classical and popular musicians may receive attractive offers to make recordings and personal appearances.

Popular and opera singers move up to better and more lucrative jobs through recognition of their talent by the public or by music producers and directors and agents. Their advancement is directly related to the demand for their talent and their own ability to promote themselves.

Music teachers in elementary and secondary schools may, with further training, aspire to careers as supervisors of music of a school system, a school district, or an entire state. With further graduate training, teachers can qualify for positions in colleges, universities, and music conservatories, where they can advance to become department heads. Well-known musicians can become artists-in-residence in the music departments of institutions of higher learning.

WHAT ARE THE SALARY RANGES?

It is difficult to estimate the earnings of the average musician, because what a musician earns is dependent upon his or her skill, reputation, geographic location, type of music, and number of engagements per year.

According to the American Federation of Musicians, musicians in the major U.S. symphony orchestras earned salaries of between $24,720 and $100,196 during the 2000-2001 performance season. The season for these major orchestras, generally located in the largest U.S. cities, ranges from 24 to 52 weeks. Featured musicians and soloists can earn much more, especially those with an international reputation. According to the U.S. Department of Labor, median annual earnings of musicians, singers, and related workers were $37,253 in 2004.

Popular musicians are usually paid per concert or gig. A band just starting out playing a small bar or club may be required to play three sets a night, and each musician may receive next to nothing for the entire evening. Often, bands receive a percentage of the cover charge at the door. Some musicians play for drinks alone. On average, however, pay per musician ranges from $30 to $300 or more per night. Bands that have gained recognition and a following may earn far more, because a club owner can usually be assured that many people will come to see the band play. The most successful popular musicians, of course, can earn millions of dollars each year.

Musicians are well paid for studio recording work, when they can get it. For recording film and television background music, musicians are paid a minimum of about $185 for a three-hour session; for record company recordings, they receive a minimum of about $235 for three hours. Instrumentalists performing live earn anywhere from $30 to $300 per engagement, depending on their degree of popularity, talent, and the size of the room they play.

According to the American Guild of Organists, full-time organists employed by religious institutions had the following salary ranges (base salary plus benefits) by educational attainment in 2006: bachelor's degree, $49,347 to $70,180; master's degree, $56,145 to $80,795; and Ph.D., $63,250 to $91,148.

The salaries received by music teachers in public elementary and secondary schools are the same as for other teachers. According to the U.S. Department of Labor, elementary and high school teachers had median yearly earnings of $43,660 and $46,120, respectively, in 2004. Music teachers in colleges and universities have widely ranging salaries. Most teachers supplement their incomes through private instruction and by performing in their off hours.

Most musicians do not, as a rule, work steadily for one employer, and they often undergo long periods of unemployment between engagements. Because of these factors, few musicians can qualify for unemployment compensation. Unlike other workers, most musicians also do not enjoy such benefits as sick leave or paid vacations. Some musicians, on the other hand, who work under contractual agreements, do receive benefits, which usually have been negotiated by artists unions, such as the American Federation of Musicians.

WHAT IS THE JOB OUTLOOK?

It is difficult to make a living solely as a musician, and this will continue because competition for jobs will be as intense as it has been in the past. Most musicians must hold down other jobs while pursuing their music careers. Thousands of musicians are all trying to make it in the music industry. Musicians are advised to be as versatile as possible, playing various kinds of music and more than one instrument. More importantly, they must be committed to pursuing their craft.

The U.S. Department of Labor predicts that employment of musicians will grow about as fast as the average through 2014. Slower-than-average employment growth is predicted for self-employed musicians. The demand for musicians will be greatest in theaters and restaurants as the public continues to spend more money on recreational activities. The outlook is also favorable for musicians in churches and

Related Jobs

- music journalists
- music librarians
- music producers
- music teachers
- music therapists
- music venue owners and managers
- music video directors and producers
- musical instrument repairers and tuners

other religious organizations. The increasing numbers of cable television networks and new television programs will likely cause an increase in employment for musicians. Digital recording technology has also made it easier and less expensive for musicians to produce and distribute their own recordings. Few musicians, however, will earn substantial incomes from these efforts. Popular musicians may receive many short-term engagements in nightclubs, restaurants, and theaters, but these engagements offer little job stability. The supply of musicians for virtually all types of music will continue to exceed the demand for the foreseeable future.

Music Librarians

SUMMARY

Definition
Music librarians help others find information and select music-related materials best suited to their needs. They are key personnel wherever books, magazines, audiovisual materials, and a variety of other informational materials are cataloged and kept.

Alternative Job Titles
None

Salary Range
$29,890 to $46,940 to $80,823+

Educational Requirements
Master's degree

Certification or Licensing
Required for certain positions

Employment Outlook
About as fast as the average

High School Subjects
Business

Computer science
Foreign language
Music

Personal Interests
Helping people: personal service
Reading/Books
Music

"One of the most interesting aspects of working in a library is how it is NOT about books," says Bradley Short, a music librarian for 19 years. "Folks often wrongly assume that much of my day is spent in quiet solitude reading new books that come to the library. Nothing could be further from the truth! In the music library, we have long had more than just books in the collection. Currently, the collection is made up of roughly one-third books, one-third sheet music (scores), and one-third sound recordings (CDs, DVDs, LPs, etc.). And, on the horizon are dozens of music magazines and journals that are now available on the Internet. Soon, the music library will have a considerable percentage of materials available electronically or over the Internet, and students and faculty will have access to materials at all hours of the day and night.

"Even still, the job of a music librarian is not about books, scores, or sound recordings. The job is about working with people. Bringing organization and clarity to a collection of materials that numbers in the millions is far beyond what any one person can do. It is only when we work together with our colleagues, to build on what work was done by previous generations of librarians, that we are able, today, to provide students and faculty with the whole array of resources that they require for a successful learning experience. The librarian's role in the educational process is a vital role but is rarely the focal point of anyone's activity. You could say that all librarians play a supporting role in this 'movie.' Understanding how to best play that role is the difference between a successful librarian working with students and faculty to meet the educational mission of the institution and a crazed stereotype of a librarian reduced to shushing noisy patrons."

WHAT DO MUSIC LIBRARIANS DO?

Music librarians perform many of the same tasks as general librarians. These duties, with an emphasis on music, include arranging, cataloging, and maintaining library collections; helping patrons find materials and advising them on how to use resources effectively; creating catalogs, indexes, brochures, exhibits, Web sites, and bibliographies to educate users about the library's resources; supervising the purchase and maintenance of the equipment needed to use these materials; hiring, training, and supervising library staff; setting and implementing budgets; and keeping abreast of developments in the field. They also select and acquire music, videotapes, records, cassettes, DVDs, compact discs, books, manuscripts, and other nonbook materials for the library; this entails evaluating newly published materials as well as seeking out older materials.

Specialized duties for music librarians vary based on their employer and their skill set. For example, a music librarian employed by a college, university, or conservatory may acquire the music needed by student musical groups, while a librarian who is employed by music publishers may help edit musical publications. Music librarians employed by radio and television stations catalog and oversee music-related materials that are used solely by employees of these organizations. They research and recommend music selections for programs, pull and refile musical selections for on-air shifts, and maintain relationships with record companies and distributors.

Some music librarians may arrange special music-related courses, presentations, or performances at their libraries. They may also compile lists of books, periodicals, articles, and audiovisual materials on music, or they may teach others how to do this.

Music librarians at large libraries may specialize in one particular task. *Music catalogers* are librarians who specialize in the cataloging and classification of music-related materials such as scores and sound recordings, software, audiovisual materials, and books. *Music bibliographers* create detailed lists of music-related materials for use by library patrons. These lists may be organized by subject, language, date, composer, musician, or other criteria.

In addition to their regular duties, some music librarians teach music- or library science-related courses at colleges and universities. Others write reviews of books and music for print and online publications.

Most libraries are pleasant and comfortable places in which to assist those doing research, studying, or reading or listening for pleasure. Music librarians must constantly read about and listen to music to keep informed in order to serve library patrons. They must also strive to stay abreast of constantly changing technology, which may seem overwhelming at times.

Some music librarians may find the work demanding and stressful when they deal with users who are working under deadline pressure. Librarians working as music catalogers may suffer eyestrain and headaches from working long hours at a computer screen.

On average, librarians work between 35 and 40 hours per week. Since most libraries are open evenings and weekends to accommodate the schedules of their users, many librarians will have a nontraditional work schedule, working, for instance, from 11:00 A.M. to 9:00 P.M., or taking Monday and Tuesday as a weekend in lieu of Saturday and Sunday.

There is, of course, some routine in library work, but the trend is to place clerical duties in the hands of library technicians and library assistants, freeing the professional music librarian for administrative, research, personnel, and community services. For the most part, music librarians tend to find the work intellec-

To Be a Successful Music Librarian, You Should . . .

- have an excellent memory
- have a keen eye for detail
- have good information-management skills
- have a love of music
- be interested in helping others
- have strong interpersonal skills if you deal with the public
- be a good problem solver

tually stimulating, challenging, and dynamic. Providing so many valuable services to the community and one's employer can be extremely rewarding.

WHAT IS IT LIKE TO BE A MUSIC LIBRARIAN?

Bradley Short has been a music librarian for 19 years. He is currently the music librarian in the St. Louis' Gaylord Music Library at Washington University. Before coming to St. Louis, he was the music and creative arts librarian at Brandeis University in Waltham, Massachusetts. "My mentor once told me that a music librarian is a classic middle-manager," he says. "In many ways this is true. Most of my day is spent implementing decisions made by the library administration or interpreting library policy to staff and patrons. This push-me/pull-you, two-headed llama approach means that most of my time is spent coordinating efforts of library personnel to accomplish library-wide goals and objectives often set by others, and then turning around and explaining to patrons why change is necessary and even desirable."

Bradley's current responsibilities are split between two jobs. He has two offices, in two different buildings, with two groups of staff to supervise. "For the past 18 months," he says, "I've been the interim acquisitions librarian as well as the music and performing arts librarian. The acquisitions librarian is in charge of overseeing book purchasing for the entire library system. It's mainly a desk job that entails working with library budgets and reports. I oversee funds for particular subjects (such as art, biology, and chemistry) and approve invoices for payment to the university business office."

Bradley arrives at the acquisitions office around 7:30 A.M. "Most university libraries are open far more hours than what any one person works," he says. "So, the first order of business is usually to respond to issues that happened while I was not there. I begin by checking e-mail and phone messages received the previous evening. For example, messages come from vendors who haven't received payment, from librarians asking about funds available for special purchases, or from donors who would like to make a gift to the library. In addition, the acquisitions unit is currently in the process of merging with another unit, so that added activity requires lots of meetings to work out the

logistics and details. Libraries are constantly changing and morphing to better respond to the needs of the university students and faculty."

Around noon, Bradley leaves the acquisition office and travels across campus to the music library. "The music library is a separate building next to the music department," he says, "and is an ideal arrangement that allows the librarians to get to know the music faculty and students much better than we could if we were in the main library building. This familiarity allows me to tailor library purchases to meet the immediate needs of the students and faculty. If I know that someone is teaching a class on Mozart or the Beatles I might spend more money purchasing books and CDs about Mozart and the Beatles rather than about Bach and jazz."

In addition to these duties, Bradley also attends committee meetings where he works with his colleagues from other parts of the library on specific projects or programs. "I've been on committees to develop a system of mentors designed to help new librarians adjust to working at Washington University; I've worked to develop promotion policies for librarians who deserve special recognition; and, I've worked with others to teach colleagues how to understand the budgeting process used by the university and how it affects the library."

Around 6 P.M., Bradley ends his workday and heads home. "I sometimes take professional reading or new catalogs home to peruse while relaxing in the evening."

DO I HAVE WHAT IT TAKES TO BE A MUSIC LIBRARIAN?

Music librarians should have an excellent memory and a keen eye for detail, as they manage a wide variety of resources. They must love music and be willing to assist others with sometimes obscure or demanding requests.

Music librarians who deal with the public should have strong interpersonal skills, tact, and patience. An imaginative, highly motivated, and resourceful personality is very valuable. An affinity for problem solving is another desirable quality. Librarians are often expected to take part in community affairs, cooperating in the preparation of exhibits, presenting book reviews, and explaining library use to community organizations. As a music librarian, you will also need to be a leader in developing the cultural and musical tastes of library patrons.

Music librarians involved with technical services should be detail-oriented, have good planning skills, and be able to think analytically. They should have a love for information and be willing to master the techniques for obtaining and presenting knowledge. Librarians must also be prepared to master constantly changing technology. "No one would have ever guessed what impact computers (let alone Google) would have on libraries back when I started college in 1976," Bradley says. "By the time I actually started working in 1987, e-mail was just becoming a reality, and the Internet as we know it today had yet to be invented. With each new change of computer system or upgrade there were new things to learn and new ways of work that needed to be adapted to. The need to adapt has been a constant throughout my career."

Finally, music librarians must be flexible and adaptable in regard to job duties and responsibilities. "As a music librarian," Bradley says, "you join the library staff as a specialist. However, a specialty can also pigeonhole someone who isn't flexible enough to understand how to continually add skills and experiences that will enhance one's contribution to the organization. The college degrees that you arrive at your first job with aren't the end of the educational process for the successful librarian. There are always new tools, or areas, or skill sets that will be needed."

HOW DO I BECOME A MUSIC LIBRARIAN?
Education

Bradley first got interested in music history as a student at Kansas State University in Manhattan, Kansas. "I had started college wanting to be a music teacher," he says, "and then added classes in music history midway through my studies. After earning my degree, I went to the University of North Carolina-Chapel Hill as a graduate student in musicology (music history). At that time, which is probably no different than it is now, the competition for college faculty positions was extremely fierce. Rather than subject myself to a potentially long string of itinerate one-year teaching positions, waiting for a tenure-track job to open, I decided to combine my love of music and the academic enterprise with the more practical and immediate needs of figuring out how to make a living. Working in libraries seemed like such an obvious choice."

High School

If you are interested in becoming a music librarian, be sure to take a full college preparatory course load. Focus on classes in music, English, speech, history, and foreign languages. Learning how to use a computer and conduct basic research in a library is essential. Developing these skills will not only aid in your future library work, but will also help you in college and in any other career areas you decide to pursue.

Bradley encourages high school students to seek out as wide a variety of music-related experiences as possible. "It may sound silly," he says, "but there is no better way to learn about music than to perform it. Students should be encouraged to participate in all kinds of ensembles—especially those that might not be the easiest for them. Instrumentalists should try out for the chorus or play in the pit for musicals. Likewise, singers should consider participating in the orchestra or learning an instrument that would allow them to join the marching band."

Postsecondary Training

Most students interested in becoming music librarians pursue undergraduate education in a music-related field. In the late 1990s, the MLA surveyed its members regarding educational achievement. The majority of its members who received a bachelor's degree in the arts or music majored in the following subjects: musicology, music education, music theory/composition, and vocal and instrumental performance.

In addition to music-related courses, be sure to take at least one foreign language since music and music literature are published in many languages. The MLA reports that the most popular foreign languages (in descending order) of its members were German, French, Italian, Spanish, Latin, and Russian. You should also take classes that strengthen your communication skills, research methods, collection organization, and customer service abilities. More than half of the accredited library schools do not require students to take introductory courses in library science while an undergraduate. It would be wise, though, to check with schools for specific requirements.

You will need to earn a master's degree to become a librarian. The degree is generally known as the master of library science (M.L.S), but in some institutions it may be referred to by a different title, such as the master of library and information science. You should plan to attend a graduate school of library and information science that is accredited by the American Library Association (ALA). Currently, there are more than 55 ALA-accredited graduate schools. Some libraries will not consider job applicants who attended a nonaccredited school.

A second master's degree in music is usually required for the best music librarianship positions. Some schools offer a dual degree in librarianship and music. Common combinations include a M.L.S. with either a master of arts in musicology, a master of music in music history, or a master of music in music theory. Other schools may allow students to take music courses that can be counted toward a library degree. Typical graduate courses include music librarianship, music bibliography, music cataloging, music libraries and information services, history of music printing, history of music documents, and special problems in music cataloging. Other graduate courses may feature sections that relate to music librarianship. Many graduate programs also offer internships or practicums in which students can gain hands-on experience working in a music library.

The Directory of Library School Offerings in Musical Librarianship, published by the Music Library Association, provides information on U.S. and Canadian library schools that offer a master's degree in library science with a concentration in music, specialized courses in music librarianship, or other music-related educational opportunities. A free, online version of the publication is available at the MLA Web site (http://www.musiclibraryassoc. org); a print version may be ordered from the association for a small fee.

A doctorate may be required for work in research libraries, university libraries, or special collections. A doctorate is commonly required for the top administrative posts of these types of libraries, as well as for faculty positions in graduate schools of library science.

Certification and Training

There is no specialized certification available for music librarians. If you plan to work outside of music librarianship as a school librarian, you are required to earn teacher's certification in addition to preparation as a librarian. You may also be required to earn a master's degree in education. Various state, county, and local governments have set up other requirements for education and certification. Contact the school board in the area in which you are interested in working for specific requirements. Your public library system should also have information readily available.

The ALA is developing voluntary certification programs to recognize individuals who have demonstrated knowledge and skills in library science and to promote professional development. Currently, it offers the certified public library administrator designation to public librarians who have at least three years of supervisory experience. For more information, visit http://www. ala-apa.org/certification/cpla.html.

Internships and Volunteerships

Most music librarianship students will be required to participate in an internship, which allows them to work closely with librarians and learn more about the field. The internship may be offered by your school's music library, by a public or private music or general library, or by another music-related organization, such as a classical music radio station or a well-known opera company. Internships typically last 4 to 12 months and

Interview: Cassidy Sugimoto

Cassidy Sugimoto is a first-year gradu-ate student in information and library science at the University of North Caro-lina-Chapel Hill. She received a bachelor of music in music performance (flute) from the university in 2005. During her undergraduate years, she worked in the university's music library at the circula-tion desk. Now she works for the music library doing special projects and in the music-cataloging department. Cassidy discussed her interest in music librarian-ship and her education with the editors of *What Can I Do Now?: Music*.

Q. Why are you interested in becom-ing a music librarian?

A. Being a music librarian is a wonderful balance of the academic, the musical, and the professional. You are able to collect, organize, and provide access to music and material about music. It is an ideal job for someone who loves music and music scholarship and wants to be surrounded by this material. In addition, it is one of the types of music careers in which you can keep a fairly stable schedule and make a decent living.

Q. What has been the most challeng-ing aspect of your education?

A. I think the most challenging aspect of my education is doing two rather disparate programs (an undergradu-ate degree in music and a graduate degree in library science) and trying to meld these two programs together. A skilled music librarian must be knowl-edgeable in both these fields, but understanding which facets of which field are necessary to music librarian-ship has been one of the most chal-lenging aspects for me.

Q. What advice would you give to high school students who are interested in this career?

A. I would encourage students to study music as their undergraduate major. Most positions in this field require at least the undergraduate degree in music (and some require advanced music degrees), so it would be advan-tageous to obtain the degree early in their career. In addition, I would encour-age students to try working in a music library as an undergraduate. You will have a much better idea of how suited you are for the career after working in the environment for a couple years.

Q. Where would you like to work once you graduate?

A. When I graduate I would like to apply for doctoral programs and get a Ph.D. in library science. I feel that there is still a considerable amount of research that could and should be done in music librarianship, and I would like to work on it. After I finish the doctorate, I would like to work as a reference librar-ian in an academic music library and teach classes in music librarianship.

are usually arranged by the school, espe-cially when the internship is a require-ment for the degree. Although most internships are unpaid, many schools offer college credit for their comple-tion.

Once you know you are interested in library work, you might be able to work as an assistant in the school library media center or find part-time work in a local public library. Such volunteer or paid positions may provide you with experience checking materials in and out at the circulation desk, shelving returned books, or typing title, subject, and author information on cards or in computer records. In college, you might be able to work as a technical or clerical assistant in your school's music library.

WHO WILL HIRE ME?

Approximately 159,000 librarians are employed in positions throughout the country. Music librarians make up a small percentage of this number. Music librarians are employed at large research libraries such as the Library of Congress; colleges, universities, and conservatories; public and private libraries; archives; radio and television stations; and musical societies and foundations. They also work for professional bands and orchestras, music publishing companies, and the military.

As the field of library and information services grows, music librarians can find more work outside the traditional library setting. Experienced music librarians may advise libraries or other agencies on information systems, library renovation projects, or other information-based issues.

Generally, music librarians must complete all educational requirements before applying for a job. In some cases, part-time work experience or an internship while in graduate school may lead to a full-time position upon graduation. Some employers, too, may allow an especially promising applicant to begin learning on the job before the library degree is conferred. As a graduate student at the University of North Carolina-Chapel Hill, Bradley got the opportunity to work in the university's music library with a collection of rare opera librettos that dated back to the 17th century. "While some of the work was routine," he recalls, "I became fascinated with the variety of work done in the library. The librarians I worked with were interesting people who had a lot to offer, not only me but to all of the students at the university."

Upon graduating, new music librarians should consult the career services offices at their school. Employers seeking new graduates often recruit through library schools. Most professional library and information science organizations have job listings that candidates can consult; for example, the MLA offers a Joblist at its Web site. Music librarians can also use online job search engines to help locate an appropriate position. Newspaper classifieds may be of some help in locating a job, although other approaches may be more appropriate to this profession.

Many music librarians entering the workforce today are combining their experience in another career with graduate library and information science education. A music teacher who plays trumpet in a band, for example, could mix her part-time teaching experience and her hobby with a degree in library science to begin a full-time career as a music librarian. Almost any music-related background can be used to advantage when entering the field of musical librarianship.

Individuals interested in working in musical library positions for the federal government can contact the human resources department—or consult the Web site—of the government agency for which they are interested in working; for these government positions, applicants must take a civil service examination. Public libraries, too, often follow a civil service system of appointment.

WHERE CAN I GO FROM HERE?

The beginning music librarian may gain experience by taking a job as an assistant. He or she can learn a lot from practical experience before attempting to manage a department or entire library. A music librarian may advance to positions with greater levels of responsibility within the same library system, or he or she may gain initial experience in a small library and then advance by transferring to a larger or more specialized library. Within a large library, promotions to higher positions are possible (for example, to the supervision of a department). Experienced music librarians with the necessary qualifications may advance to positions in library administration, such as *library director,* who is at the head of a typical library organizational scheme. This professional sets library policies and plans and administers programs of library services, usually under the guidance of a governing body, such as a board of directors or board of trustees. Library directors

have overall responsibility for the operation of a library system. A doctorate is desirable for reaching top administrative levels, as well as for landing a graduate library school faculty position.

Experienced music librarians, in particular those with strong administrative, computer, or planning backgrounds, may move into the area of information consulting. They use their expertise to advise libraries and other organizations on issues regarding information services. Other experienced librarians, especially those with computer experience, may also go into specialized areas of library work, becoming increasingly valuable to business and industry, as well as other fields.

WHAT ARE THE SALARY RANGES?

Salaries for music librarians depend on such factors as the location, size, and type of library, the amount of experience the librarian has, and the responsibilities of the position. According to the U.S. Department of Labor, median annual earnings of all librarians in 2004 were $46,940. Salaries ranged from less than $29,890 to more than $71,270. Librarians working in colleges and universities earned $51,550. Librarians employed in local government earned $45,220. In the federal government, the average salary for all librarians was $67,850 in 2004.

The American Library Association's Survey of Librarian Salaries reports the following mean salaries for librarians and managers in 2004: library directors, $80,823; deputy/associate/assistant directors, $66,497; managers/supervisors of support staff, $56,690; librarians who do not supervise, $45,554; and beginning librarians, $38,918.

Most music librarians receive a full benefits package, which may include paid vacation time, holiday pay, compensated sick leave, various insurance plans, and retirement savings programs. Librarians who work in a college or university library may receive tuition waivers to help them earn advanced degrees in their field.

WHAT IS THE JOB OUTLOOK?

The ALA predicts a serious shortage of librarians in the next 5 to 12 years. The association reports that one in four librarians is expected to retire in the next 5 to 7 years, and approximately half will retire within 12 years.

Employment prospects for music librarians will not be as strong. The field of musical librarianship is small, and there is little turnover in the best positions. Music librarians with advanced education and knowledge of more than one foreign language will have the best employment prospects. Employment opportunities will also arise for music librarians who have a background in information science and library automation. The rapidly expanding field of information management has created a demand for qualified people to set up and maintain information systems for private industry and consulting firms.

Related Jobs

- archivists
- book conservators
- conservators and conservation technicians
- database managers
- information brokers
- library media specialists
- library technicians
- museum directors and curators
- music teachers
- museum technicians
- musicians

Music Teachers

SUMMARY

Definition
Music teachers instruct people on how to sing, play musical instruments, and appreciate and enjoy the world of music.

Alternative Job Titles
Music educators

Salary Range
$19,000 to $49,740 to $85,230+

Educational Requirements
Bachelor's degree

Certification or Licensing
Voluntary (certification)
Required for certain positions (licensing)

Employment Outlook
About as fast as the average

High School Subjects
Music

Psychology
Speech

Personal Interests
Entertaining/performing
Music
Teaching

Imelda Kaminski, a music teacher for 50 years, is always looking for new music ideas. "For a recent concert," she recalls, "I wanted the students to play anthems from different countries. I contacted different embassies and airlines for help, but finally found a book of anthems at the local library. Since the music provided was written for the piano, I had to change the arrangements for the violins."

Imelda eventually found the music to match the ethnicities of her students, purchased country flags, and asked students to wear ethnic costumes to the concert—which was a great success. "This concert taught students about different countries and their anthems, but more importantly, the fact that though we are different, we are also the same."

WHAT DOES A MUSIC TEACHER DO?

Music teachers help students learn to read music, develop their voices, breathe correctly, and hold and play their instruments properly. As their students master the techniques of their art, teachers guide them through more and more difficult pieces of music. Music teachers often organize recitals or concerts that feature their students. These recitals allow family and friends to hear how well the students are progressing and help students get performing experience.

Elementary school music teachers teach basic music concepts and simple instruments to students, gradually adding more advanced topics or instrument instruction. They teach introductory lessons in music reading, music appreciation, and vocal and instrumental music. They may organize musical programs for pageants, plays, and other school events.

Secondary school music teachers teach music history, music appreciation, music theory, and other music-related courses to students in group and/or one-on-one lessons. They also teach students how to play percussion, wind, and string instruments. They direct in-school glee clubs, concert choirs, choral groups, marching bands, or orchestras. Since music is usually an elective at the high school level, music teachers often work with students who have some musical knowledge or ability.

College and university music teachers are also frequently performers or composers. They divide their time between group and individual instruction and may teach several music subjects, such as music appreciation and music history, arrangement, composition, conducting, theory, and pedagogy (the teaching of music). They use lectures, quizzes and tests, listening exercises in a musical laboratory, and performance before a jury (a group of faculty music teachers) to educate and assess the abilities of their students.

Private music teachers, also known as *studio music teachers,* may teach children who are just beginning to play or sing, teens who hope to make music their career, or adults who are interested in music lessons for their own enjoyment. They teach these students in a studio, in their homes, or at their students' homes. Private music teachers who teach music to very young children are sometimes known as *early childhood music educators.*

In addition to teaching students, music teachers also perform administrative tasks, such as assessing and grading the performance of their students, keeping attendance records, ordering supplies, storing and maintaining musical instruments and other classroom materials, and meeting with parents to discuss the performance of their children. They also plan classroom lessons based on local or state requirements and the National Standards for Music Education.

To earn extra income, music teachers may also direct school musicals or community choirs or other musical groups, work in community theater, or perform as musicians or singers. Some music teachers also work as freelance music writers, composers and arrangers, and in other music-related professions.

WHAT IS IT LIKE TO BE A MUSIC TEACHER?

Imelda Kaminski has taught violin, cello, and piano for 50 years. She teaches both from her home music studio and at a community college in Palos Hills, Illinois. In addition to teaching, she has also worked in sales, instrument repair, and recruitment of students. "By the time I was in 8th grade, I already knew how to play the violin, cello, and piano," Imelda says. "But in the 6th grade, a nun I studied with inspired me to become a music instructor."

Imelda teaches children's classes at the community college each Saturday. "I am usually at the college an hour before classes start and teach classes back to back," she says, "with little or no break

time. I also teach students at my home studio." Most days she teaches classes in the morning, afternoon, and at night. Imelda currently teaches 100 students at the community college and 65 students at home, but that number fluctuates from semester to semester. "My classes at the college vary in size, since I cannot control the size of each class," she says. "If needed, I will split a class to accommodate the age and experience of the students. I like a smaller class, since there is more hands-on instruction."

Imelda works more than 60 hours a week. "I spend as much time looking for new music as I do teaching it!" she says. "I attend the Midwest Band and Orchestra clinic each December, where I take part in teaching workshops, as well as research music provided by publishing companies and music manufacturers." Imelda also plays at weddings, funerals, luncheons, and other events. "I do not advertise my services," she says, "but usually get these contracts through word of mouth."

DO I HAVE WHAT IT TAKES TO BE A MUSIC TEACHER?

Above all, music teachers must have a broad cultural background and a love for music. They should be proficient with at least one musical instrument or demonstrate strong vocal ability. Many feel that the desire to teach is a calling. This calling is based on a love of learning. Teachers of young children and young adults must respect their students as individuals, with personalities, strengths, and

Pros and Cons

We asked Imelda Kaminski to tell us what she liked best and least about working as a music teacher:

PROS:

- There is great satisfaction in teaching. For example, we had a young lady with a learning disability who started with us at about 5 years of age. By the time she was 18 years old, she was playing in a suburban symphony.

- Music teachers can truly make a difference in someone's life. It's rewarding to be able to draw the gift of music out of someone.

CONS:

- The hours are long, and you do not receive much pay for the hours you work.

- When working as a private teacher, or part-time instructor at a school, there are no benefits.

- Many times, the music program at a school is the first program eliminated due to financial cutbacks.

weaknesses of their own. "When teaching very young students, you must remember to be patient," Imelda advises. "The student is a child, not a miniature adult. Remember, if all students already know how to play well, you wouldn't have a job."

Music teachers must also be patient and self-disciplined to manage a large group independently. Because they work with students who are at very impressionable ages, music teachers should serve as good role models. Elementary and secondary teachers should also be well organized, as they have to keep track of the work and progress of many students.

If you aim to teach at the college level, you should enjoy reading, writing, researching, and performing. Not only will you spend many years studying in school, but your whole career will be based on communicating your thoughts and ideas. People skills are important because you'll be dealing directly with students, administrators, and other faculty members on a daily basis. You should feel comfortable in a role of authority and possess self-confidence in your teaching and musical abilities.

HOW DO I BECOME A MUSIC TEACHER?

Education

Imelda has a background in music, as well as training in Suzuki instruction. "I teach Suzuki as a method," she explains, "but also incorporate other music as part of the instruction. Most colleges today will look for instructors with at least a master's degree if teaching an accredited music class."

High School

If you are interested in becoming a music teacher, you probably are already taking voice lessons or are learning to play an instrument in high school. Participation in music classes, choral groups, bands, and orchestras is also good preparation for a music teaching career.

Postsecondary Training

Like all musicians, music teachers spend years mastering their instruments or developing their voices. Private teachers need no formal training or licenses, but most have spent years studying with an experienced musician, either in a school or conservatory or through private lessons. Teachers in elementary schools and high schools must have at least a bachelor's degree in music education as well as a state-issued teaching license. Approximately 600 conservatories, universities, and colleges offer bachelor's degrees in music education to qualify students for state certificates. The National Association of Schools of Music offers a directory of accredited music schools at its Web site, http://nasm.arts-accredit.org.

To teach music in colleges and schools of music or in conservatories, you must usually have a graduate degree in music. Many teachers at this level also have doctorate degrees. However, very talented and well-known performers or composers are sometimes hired without any formal graduate training, but only a few people reach that level of fame.

> ## To Be a Successful Music Teacher, You Should . . .
>
> - have a broad cultural background and a love of music
> - be proficient with at least one musical instrument or demonstrate strong vocal ability
> - have a love of learning and teaching
> - be able to respect your students as individuals
> - be patient, self-disciplined, and well organized
> - be able to market your abilities to potential students
> - be able to communicate your thoughts and ideas to students of various ages
> - have confidence in your teaching and musical abilities

Certification and Training

The Music Teachers National Association (MTNA) offers voluntary certification to music teachers who meet academic, performance, and teaching competencies and pass proficiency examinations in music theory, music history/literature, and/or pedagogy/teaching education. Upon fulfillment of these requirements, the applicant may use the designation *nationally certified teacher of music*. Contact the MTNA for more information on certification.

Elementary and secondary music teachers who work in public schools must be licensed under regulations estab-lished by the state in which they are teaching. If moving, teachers have to comply with any other regulations in their new state to be able to teach, though many states have reciprocity agreements that make it easier for teachers to change locations.

Licensure examinations test prospective teachers for competency in basic subjects such as reading, writing, teaching, and other subject matter. In addition, many states are moving toward a performance-based evaluation for licensing. In this case, after passing the teaching examination, prospective teachers are given provisional licenses. Only after proving themselves capable in the classroom are they eligible for a full license.

Another growing trend spurred by recent teacher shortages in elementary and high schools is alternative licensure arrangements. Some states are issuing provisional licenses to aspiring teachers who have bachelor's degrees but lack formal education courses and training in the classroom. These workers immediately begin teaching under the supervision of a licensed educator for one to two years and take education classes outside of their working hours. Once they have completed the required course work and gained experience in the classroom, they are granted a full license.

Internships and Volunteerships

College music education students typically are required to work as student teachers in order to gain experience and receive feedback regarding their teaching abilities. Contact your college's department of education for more information on student teaching opportunities.

If you are an especially talented musician, you might offer free or low-cost lessons to neighborhood children interested in learning more about music. To gain general teaching experience, look for leadership opportunities that involve working with children. You might find summer work as a counselor in a summer music camp, as a leader of a scout troop, or as an assistant in a public park or community center. To get firsthand teaching experience, volunteer for a peer-tutoring program. Many other teaching opportunities may exist in your community.

Labor Unions

Teachers who are employed by elementary, secondary, and postsecondary institutions may belong to unions such as the American Federation of Teachers and the National Education Association.

WHO WILL HIRE ME?

There are more than 2.6 million elementary and secondary school teachers employed in the United States. Music teachers make up a very small percentage of this group. The largest number of teaching positions are available in urban or suburban areas, but career opportunities also exist in small towns. Music teachers are also finding opportunities in charter schools, which are smaller, deregulated schools that receive public funding.

There are approximately 65,600 college and university music, art, and drama professors in the United States. According to the U.S. Department of Labor, the following states have the highest concentrations of college music teachers: Massachusetts, Washington, and Minnesota. With a doctorate, a number of publications or notable performances, and a record of good teaching, music professors should find opportunities in universities all across the country.

Elementary and secondary school music teachers can use their college placement offices and state departments of education to find job openings. Many local schools advertise teaching positions in newspapers. Another option is to directly contact the administration of the schools at which you'd like to work. While looking for a full-time position, you can work as a substitute teacher. In more urban areas with many schools, you may be able to find full-time substitute work.

Prospective college professors should start the process of finding a teaching position while in graduate school. You will need to develop a curriculum vita (a detailed, academic resume), work on your academic writing, assist with research, attend conferences, demonstrate your musical ability, and gain teaching experience and recommendations. Because of the competition for tenure-track positions, you may have to work for a few years in temporary positions. Some professional associations maintain lists of teaching opportunities in their areas. They may also make lists of applicants available to college administrators looking to fill an available position.

MENC: The National Association for Music Education offers job listings at its Web site, http://www.menc.org. Association members can also register as job seekers at the site.

WHERE CAN I GO FROM HERE?

As elementary and secondary music teachers acquire experience or additional education, they earn higher wages and are assigned more responsibilities. Teachers with leadership skills and an interest in administrative work may advance to serve as principals or supervisors, though the number of these positions is limited and competition for them is fierce. Another move may be into higher education, teaching music classes at a community college or university. For most of these positions, additional education is required. Other common career transitions are into related fields.

At the college level, the normal pattern of advancement is from instructor to assistant professor, to associate professor, to full professor. All four academic ranks are concerned primarily with teaching and research. College faculty members who have an interest in and a talent for administration may be advanced to chair of a department or to dean of their college. A few become college or university presidents or other types of administrators.

Private music teachers advance by establishing reputations as excellent teachers, which increases the number of students interested in studying with them.

WHAT ARE THE SALARY RANGES?

Music teachers earn a wide range of salaries based on their level of expertise, geographic location, whether they work full time or part time, and other factors. According to the National Association for Music Education, early childhood music educators earn $6 to $60/hour, while studio music teachers earn $10 to $100/hour. Full-time music teachers at the elementary and secondary levels earn salaries that range from $19,000 to $70,000 annually.

College professors' earnings vary depending on their academic department, the size of the school, the type of school (public, private, women's only, etc.), and the level of position the professor holds. The U.S. Department of Labor reports that college music, art, and drama teach-

---

Related Jobs

- child care workers
- child life specialists
- composers and arrangers
- guidance counselors
- music journalists and writers
- music therapists
- musical directors and conductors
- musicians
- singers
- teacher aides

ers earned median annual salaries of $49,740 in 2004. The lowest-paid teachers in this group earned less than $28,010, and the highest paid earned $85,230 or more annually. Postsecondary music teachers in California, Rhode Island, New York, the District of Columbia, and Connecticut earned the highest salaries.

WHAT IS THE JOB OUTLOOK?

After decades of program declines, music education is regaining popularity in U.S. schools. In 2000, a Gallup Poll found that 93 percent of Americans believed that music should be part of school curricula—a 5 percent increase from 1997. As a result, career opportunities in teaching music are expected to be good at the elementary and secondary levels. Although music programs are on the rebound in many schools, some public schools facing severe budget problems are still eliminating music programs, making competition for jobs at these schools even keener. In addition, private music teachers are facing greater competition from instrumental musicians who increasingly must turn to teaching because of the oversupply of musicians seeking playing jobs.

Though the *Occupational Outlook Handbook* predicts much-faster-than-average employment growth for college and university professors through 2014, music teachers will experience strong competition for full-time, tenure-track positions at four-year schools. Music educators who aspire to teach at the college level will enjoy the strongest employment prospects at community colleges.

Music Therapists

SUMMARY

Definition
Music therapists use music to treat and rehabilitate people with mental, physical, and emotional disabilities.

Alternative Job Titles
None

Salary Range
$15,000 to $38,816 to $100,000

Educational Requirements
Bachelor's degree

Certification or Licensing
Required

Employment Outlook
About as fast as the average

High School Subjects
Music
Psychology

Personal Interests
Helping people: emotionally
Music

WHAT DOES A MUSIC THERAPIST DO?

Similar to dreaming, creative arts therapy taps into the subconscious and gives people a mode of expression in an uncensored environment. This is important because before patients can begin to heal, they must first identify their feelings. Once they recognize their feelings, they can begin to develop an understanding of the relationship between their feelings and their behavior.

Music therapists use musical lessons and activities to improve a patient's self-confidence and self-awareness, to relieve states of depression, and to improve physical dexterity. For example, a music therapist treating a patient with Alzheimer's disease might play songs from the patient's past in order to stimulate long- and short-term memory, soothe feelings of agitation, and increase a sense of reality. A musical therapist treating a patient with a physical disability may have the patient play a keyboard or xylophone to improve their dexterity or have them walk to a musical selection to improve their balance and gait. Music therapists also treat people with mental health needs, learning and developmental disabilities, physical disabilities, brain injuries, conditions related to aging, alcohol and drug abuse problems, and acute and chronic pain.

The main goal of a music therapist is to improve the client's physical, mental, and emotional health. Before therapists begin any treatment, they meet with a team of other health care professionals. After determining the strengths, limitations, and interests of their client, they create a program to promote positive change and growth. The music therapist continues to confer with the other health care workers as the program progresses and adjusts the program according to the client's response to the therapy.

Patients undergoing music therapy do not need to have any special musical ability or be open to one particular musical style. Of course, the patient's personal therapy preferences, physical and mental circumstances, and his or her taste in music (such as a fondness for rap, classical, or country music) will all affect how the music therapist treats the patient.

Music therapists work with all age groups: young children, adolescents, adults, and senior citizens. They work in individual, group, or family sessions. The approach of the therapist, however, depends on the specific needs of the client or group.

Some music therapists may also edit or write publications about music or creative arts therapy, work as professional musicians, or specialize in other creative arts therapy careers such as art, dance, or drama therapy. Others, such as Marie Digiammarino, the director of music therapy at Illinois State University, teach music therapy education courses at colleges and universities. "I began my music career as a music educator in a rural school district," she says. "I provided general music classes to all students in grades K through 6 and special education, and also conducted the junior and senior high choirs. The special education class

To Be a Successful Music Therapist, You Should . . .

- be patient, caring, and have a genuine interest in others
- be musically proficient
- be committed to all aspects of the treatment process
- have good communication skills
- be able to work well with other people
- have a good sense of humor

responded so well to music, and I enjoyed the class so much, I decided to explore music therapy." After completing her master's degree in music education, and earning music therapy certification, Marie provided music therapy for children with mental retardation in state-run institutions for a number of years. "I was hired as the director of music therapy at Illinois State University in 1981 and later, completed a doctorate in special education. I continue to direct the music therapy program at Illinois State University, teaching classes and serving as an advisor to music therapy students."

WHAT IS IT LIKE TO BE A MUSIC THERAPIST?

Music therapists work a typical 40-hour, five-day workweek; at times, however, they may have to work extra hours. The number of patients under a therapist's care depends on their specific employment setting. Although many therapists work in hospitals, they may also be employed in such facilities as clinics, rehabilitation centers, children's homes, schools, and nursing homes. Some therapists maintain service contracts with several facilities. For instance, a therapist might work two days a week at a hospital, one day at a nursing home, and the rest of the week at a rehabilitation center. This type of work arrangement entails frequent travel from location to location to see patients.

Most buildings are pleasant, comfortable, and clean places in which to work. Experienced music therapists might choose to be self-employed, working with patients in their own studios. In such a case, the therapist might work more irregular hours to accommodate patient schedules. Other therapists might maintain a combination of service contract work with one or more facilities in addition to a private caseload of clients referred to them by other health care professionals. Whether therapists work on service contracts with various facilities or maintain private practices, they must handle all of the business and administrative details and worries that go along with being self-employed.

DO I HAVE WHAT IT TAKES TO BE A MUSIC THERAPIST?

"A music therapist must be patient, caring, and have a genuine interest in other people," says Marie Digiammarino. "A music therapist must be musically proficient in order to use live music in interactions with others, and have good writing skills to document and communicate treatment effectiveness. They also must be committed to all aspects of the treatment process: assessment, planning, treatment implementation, and documentation. A music therapist must have good interaction skills to work collaboratively with other team members."

You must have the patience and the stamina to teach and practice therapy with patients for whom progress is often very slow because of their various physical and emotional disorders. A therapist must always keep in mind that even a tiny amount of progress might be extremely significant for some patients and their families. A good sense of humor is also a valuable trait.

HOW DO I BECOME A MUSIC THERAPIST?
Education
High School

To become a music therapist, you will need a bachelor's degree, so take a college preparatory curriculum while in high school. You should become as proficient as possible with music, musical instruments, and musical theory. When therapists work with patients, they must be able to concentrate completely on the patient rather than on learning how to use tools or techniques. A good starting point for an aspiring music therapist is to study piano or guitar.

A Short History of Music Therapy

Creative arts therapy programs are fairly recent additions to the health care field. Although many theories of mental and physical therapy have existed for centuries, it has been only in the last 70 years or so that health care professionals have truly realized the healing powers of music and other forms of artistic self-expression.

According to the American Music Therapy Association (AMTA), the discipline of music therapy began during World War I, when amateur and professional musicians visited veteran's hospitals to play for the thousands of veterans who were being treated for both physical and emotional maladies caused by the war. Health administrators and physicians recognized that the music positively affected their patients, and music therapists were hired to formally work with patients. The field of music therapy advanced further during and after World War II, when the Department of Veterans Affairs (VA) developed and organized various music and other creative arts activities for patients in VA hospitals. These activities had a dramatic effect on the physical and mental well-being of the veterans, and music and other creative arts therapists began to be used to help treat and rehabilitate patients in other health care settings.

As music therapy grew in popularity, it became evident that formal training was needed for music therapists to be most effective. The first music therapy degree program in the world was founded at Michigan State University in 1944. Today, there are more than 70 AMTA-approved music therapy programs in the United States.

In 1998, the AMTA was founded as a result of a merger between the National Association for Music Therapy and the American Association for Music Therapy. Its oversight of educational programs ensures the professional integrity of music therapists working in the field.

In addition to courses such as drama, music, and English, you should consider taking introductory classes in psychology. Also, communications classes will give you an understanding of the various ways people communicate, both verbally and nonverbally.

Postsecondary Training

To become a music therapist, you must earn at least a bachelor's degree in music therapy. There are more than 70 AMTA-approved college and university music therapy programs in the United States. Typical courses in a bachelor's degree program in music therapy include professional music therapy, music therapy theory, assessment, evaluation, populations served, ethics, and research and clinical interventions. Undergraduates will also take supporting courses in music, psychology, and human physiology.

In most cases, however, you will also need a graduate degree to advance in the field. Graduate school admissions requirements vary by program, so you would be wise to contact the graduate programs you are interested in to find out about their admissions policies. For some fields, you may be required to submit a portfolio of your work along with the written application. The AMTA provides a list of schools that meet its quality standards at its Web site, http://www.musictherapy.org/handbook/schools.html.

In graduate school, your study of psychology and music will be in-depth. Classes for someone seeking a master's in music therapy may include group psychotherapy, foundation of creativity theory, assessment and treatment planning, and music therapy presentation. In addition to classroom study, you will complete an internship or supervised practicum (that is, work with clients). Depending on your program, you may also need to write a thesis or present a final artistic project before receiving your degree.

Certification and Training

Students who receive a bachelor's degree in music therapy are eligible to sit for a certification examination offered by the Certification Board for Music Therapists. Therapists who successfully complete this examination may use the designation *music therapist–board certified*. Music therapists are required to renew this certification every five years by completing continuing education credits or by retaking the certification exam.

Many music therapists hold additional licenses in other fields, such as social work, education, mental health, or marriage and family therapy. In some states, music therapists need to be licensed, depending on

their place of work. For specific information on licensing, you will need to check with your state's licensing board. In addition to membership in the AMTA, music therapists are usually members of other professional associations, including the American Psychological Association, the American Association of Marriage and Family Therapy, and the American Counseling Association.

Internships and Volunteerships

Music therapy students are usually required to participate in an internship or clinical experience as part of their educational training in an approved mental health, special education, or health care facility. For example, program requirements in the music therapy program at Illinois State University (ISU) consist of two different levels of field experience. "The first level," explains Marie Digiammarino, "occurs while students are still taking on-campus courses. Students are assigned four different clinical experiences during their junior and senior years, providing music to special populations in the community." Field experience sites for ISU's program include special education classes serving students with physical, hearing, and visual impairments, mental retardation, and behavior disorders; a juvenile detention center; a hospital unit serving adolescents and adults with mental health problems; nursing homes; and hospice. "The second level of field experience is a six-month (40-hour-per-week) music therapy internship students begin after all of their on-campus academic course work is complete," says Marie. "Students apply for the internship like applying for a job, to sites all over the country that are approved by the American Music Therapy Association. Students compete for these sites with music therapy students from all over the country. As part of the application process, students may be asked to provide transcripts, letters of recommendation, and resumes. In order to be competitive, maintaining high grades during college is important. After students have completed all required courses, including the six-month music therapy internship, they are eligible to take the Certification Board for Music Therapists exam." Visit the AMTA's Web site (http://www.musictherapy.org/handbook/ctindex.html) for comprehensive information on internships.

To learn more about careers in music therapy, visit the Web site of the AMTA. Talk with people working in the music therapy field and try to arrange to observe a music therapy session. Look for part-time or summer jobs, or volunteer at a hospital, clinic, nursing home, or any of a number of health care facilities. You might also consider becoming a student member of the AMTA. As a membership benefit, you will receive association publications such as the *Journal of Music Therapy* and *Music Therapy Perspectives.*

A summer job as an aide at a camp for disabled children, for example, may help provide insight into the nature of music therapy, including both its rewards and its demands. Such experience can be very valuable in deciding if you are suited to handle the inherent frustrations of a therapy career.

WHO WILL HIRE ME?

Music therapists usually work as members of an interdisciplinary health care team that may include physicians, nurses, social workers, psychiatrists, and psychologists. Although often employed in medical and psychiatric hospitals, therapists also work in rehabilitation centers, nursing homes, day treatment facilities, shelters for battered women, pain and stress management clinics, substance abuse programs, hospices, and correctional facilities. Others maintain their own private practices. Some music therapists work with children in grammar and high schools, either as therapists or as music teachers. Others teach or conduct research in the creative arts at colleges and universities. "Be aware," advises Marie Digiammarino, "that music therapists can be hired under a variety of job titles, such as music therapist, activity therapist, creative arts therapist, expressive arts therapist, and other titles."

Unpaid training internships (see the AMTA Web site for a list of internship opportunities) or assistantships that students complete during study for a bachelor's degree in music therapy often can lead to a first job in the field. Graduates can use the career services offices at their colleges or universities to help them find positions in the field. AMTA members can also access a list of job openings at the association's Web site. "Become a member of the music therapy profession on the national, regional, and state levels," Marie advises, "as most of these organizations maintain job listings."

Music therapists who are new to the field might consider doing volunteer work at a nonprofit community organization, correctional facility, or neighborhood association to gain some practical experience. Therapists who want to start their own practice can host group therapy sessions in their homes. Music therapists may also wish to associate with other members of the alternative health care field in order to gain experience and build a client base.

WHERE CAN I GO FROM HERE?

With experience, music therapists can move into supervisory, administrative, and teaching positions. Often, the supervision of interns can resemble a therapy session. The interns will discuss their feelings and ask questions they may have regarding their work with clients. How did they handle their clients? What were the reactions to what their clients said or did? What could they be doing to help more? The supervising therapist helps the interns become competent music therapists.

WHAT ARE THE SALARY RANGES?

Salaries for music therapists vary based on experience, level of training, and education. Music therapists earned average annual salaries of $38,816 in 2001, according to the AMTA. Salaries reported by AMTA members ranged from $15,000 to $100,000.

According to MENC: The National Association for Music Education, music therapists earn the following annual salaries based on employment setting: hospital psychiatric facility, $20,000 to $62,000; special education facility, $22,000 to $42,000; clinic for disabled children, $15,000 to $70,000; mental health center, $21,000 to $65,000; nursing home, $17,000 to $65,000; correctional facility, $23,000 to $58,000; and private practice, $18,000 to $77,000.

Music therapists in private practice must provide their own benefits, including health insurance.

WHAT IS THE JOB OUTLOOK?

The AMTA predicts a promising future for the field of music therapy. Demand for music therapists will increase as medical professionals and the general public become aware of the benefits gained

---

Related Jobs

- art therapists
- bibliotherapists
- creative arts therapists
- dance/movement therapists
- drama therapists
- horticultural therapists
- hypnotherapists
- music teachers
- poetry therapists
- social workers

through music therapy. Although enrollment in college therapy programs is increasing, new graduates are usually able to find jobs. In cases where an individual is unable to find a full-time position, a therapist might obtain service contracts for part-time work at several facilities.

Job openings in facilities such as nursing homes should continue to increase as the elderly population grows over the next few decades. Advances in medical technology and the recent practice of early discharge from hospitals should also create new opportunities in managed care facilities, chronic pain clinics, cancer care facilities, and hospices. The demand for music therapists should continue to increase as more people become aware of the need to help patients with disabilities and the ill in creative ways.

Music Video Directors and Producers

SUMMARY

Definition
Music video directors oversee the creative aspects of the production of a music video. Music video producers often work with the music video director by managing the budget, production schedule, and other tasks associated with music video production.

Alternative Job Titles
None

Salary Range
$26,940 to $89,410 to $120,000+

Educational Requirements
High school diploma

Certification or Licensing
None available

Employment Outlook
About as fast as the average

High School Subjects
Business

Computer science
Music
Theater

Personal Interests
Entertaining/performing
Film and television
Music
Selling/making a deal
Theater

Music video producers have greater control over their working conditions than most other people working in the music video industry. They may have the autonomy of setting their own hours and, when necessary, delegating duties to others. The work often brings considerable personal satisfaction, but it is not without constraints. Producers must work within a stressful schedule complicated by competing work pressures and often daily crises. Long hours and weekend work are common. "The hours can be very long," says Catherine Finkenstaedt, a music video producer in Los Angeles, California. "There's never a set amount of hours; it just takes what it takes on my part. Of course, when we shoot we are limited to a specific period since time definitely costs money. But since I oversee everything, sometimes I don't sleep, but I still love it!"

WHAT DO MUSIC VIDEO DIRECTORS AND PRODUCERS DO?

Music video directors and producers often work together as a team to create music videos for record companies and other employers. (Occasionally, a director may be responsible for all of the producer's tasks.) Though the director and producer work as a team, they generally approach their collaborative effort from two distinct vantage points. In short, the director is concerned with aesthetic issues such as the look, feel, and sound of the video. Directors bear the ultimate responsibility for the tone and quality of the videos they work on. They are involved in preproduction (before the shoot), production (during the shoot), and postproduction (after the shoot). The producer is concerned with more practical concerns such as electricity and catering, logistics, and business-related issues.

To be considered for jobs, music video directors and producers must present a bid (a written estimate of how much money they will need to shoot and complete the video) and a treatment to music recording executives, most often a video commissioner or marketing director. A treatment is a written overview of what a director plans to do in the music video. This is the director's only opportunity to convince music industry executives that he or she is the right person for the job. Some music video directors write only one treatment for a video, while others write three or more treatments and choose what they think is the best one for submission. Music video treatments are typically two pages long and answer questions such as: How will the video look and feel? What story will the video tell to viewers? Will the video feature music performance only, a story only, or a combination of the two? What type of medium will be used to shoot the music video: 16 mm film, 35 mm film, video, or a combination of several formats? During this time, the director and producer meet with the *music video editor*, who shares their vision about the music video. They discuss the objectives of the video and the various ways to best present the artist's image, including settings, scenes, special effects, costumes, and camera angles.

After the director and producer submit the treatment, record industry executives review it and suggest revisions based on the project's budget and stylistic concerns. The director and producer then submit a revised treatment that is reviewed, and eventually approved, by the video commissioner, marketing director, music artist's manager, and the artist. Once a treatment is accepted, the director and producer begin work on the music video within days or weeks.

Music video directors are responsible for many tasks before and during the shoot. They interpret the stories and narratives presented in scripts and coordinate the filming of their interpretations. To do this, the director creates a shooting script and storyboards as a guide to assist in making the video. Music video directors must audition, select, and rehearse the acting crew, which may include dancers, actors, stunt performers, and backup musicians, as well as work closely with the musical artist in the video. They oversee set designs and costumes and decide where scenes should be shot, what backgrounds might be needed, and how special effects can be used. Directors might also book crew members, hire vendors, and ensure that gear and locations are secured. Music video producers may handle some of these tasks so that the director can focus on the more artistic aspects of the production.

Music video directors are occasionally assisted by *directors of photography (DPs),* or *cinematographers,* who are responsible for organizing and implementing the actual camera work. The director and the DP interpret scenes and decide on appropriate camera motion to achieve desired results. The DP determines the amounts of natural and artificial lighting required for each shoot and such technical factors as the type of film to be used, camera angles and distance, depth of field, and focus.

To Be a Successful Music Video Director, You Should . . .

- have a strong creative vision for your projects
- have strong communication skills
- be able to work well with others
- be a good manager of time and talent
- be willing to work under tight production deadlines
- have a love of music
- have good knowledge of music videos and the narrative forms necessary to create them

To Be a Successful Music Video Producer, You Should . . .

- have strong business acumen
- be able to work well with others
- have a keen sense for what projects will be artistically and commercially successful
- be detail-oriented
- be a good problem-solver

Music videos, like motion pictures, are usually filmed out of sequence, meaning that the ending might be shot first and scenes from the middle of the video might not be filmed until the end of production. Directors are responsible for scheduling each day's sequence of scenes. They coordinate filming so that scenes using the same set and performers will be filmed together. In addition to conferring with the producer and the DP (if one is used during the shoot), music video directors meet with technicians and crew members to advise on and approve final scenery, lighting, props, and other necessary equipment. They are also involved with final approval of costumes and choreography.

After all the scenes have been shot, postproduction begins. The director and producer work with picture and sound editors to create the final product. The music video editor assembles shots according to the wishes of the director and producer and his or her own artistic sensibility, synchronizing film with voice and sound tracks produced by the sound editor and music editor.

When the music video is complete, the director and producer submit it to their employer (such as a record company, a production company, etc.) for final review. The employer may return the video for tweaking or major revisions. The video is revised and resubmitted until it meets the approval of the employer.

While music video directors and producers supervise all major aspects of music video production, various assistants—especially in big-budget productions—help throughout the process. In a less creative position than the director, the *first assistant director* organizes various practical matters involved during the shooting of each scene. The *second assistant director* is a coordinator who works as a liaison among the production office, the first assistant director, and the performers.

WHAT IS IT LIKE TO BE A MUSIC VIDEO DIRECTOR OR PRODUCER?

Catherine Finkenstaedt is an executive producer at The Mine, a small production company in Los Angeles, California. She has been executive producing for nearly 15 years. She starts her workday very early since her company conducts a lot of business with companies on the East Coast and in Europe. "My main responsibility is overseeing projects from the time the track of music crosses my desk through to postproduction," she explains. "So, to generally explain what happens to get a music video done:

"I represent directors who are exclusive to my company. I have signed these directors based on different aspects of their work that appealed to me, and which I felt I could fully support. Each director's work applies to different styles of music. For example, one director may have a demo reel that is more rock, and one director might have one that is more pop, and so on. When there is an appropriate track for one of my directors, the client, known as the video commissioner, will send it to me with what we call a 'brief,' which describes what they are looking for in the video (e.g., more performance- oriented, make the lead singer a rock star, or create a performance with some narrative element). Sometimes the band themselves will have a very specific idea, and the director is asked to help interpret that idea in a way that translates well to film. We are also told how much money they want to spend in total on the video.

"The director then listens to the track and hopefully gets inspired and writes up an idea. The ability to write is a very, very important skill for directors to develop. I then submit the idea to the video commissioner. The video commissioner then circulates it to everyone on his or her end who has a say—the promotions department, the band's manager, and the band. If they like the idea, they'll come back to me and ask me to budget out the costs to shoot the idea. I'll then do a budget and submit that.

"If everything comes together, they will come back and give me the job for the director. But the process is far from over. Then it's my responsibility to speak with the director about the creative approach: locations or stage, what director of photography would be best, what kind of styling for the band, how extensive is the art department, and so on. I then hire a freelance producer to come in and put it all together whilst I oversee everything.

"We then shoot the video and go into postproduction. This involves transferring the film we have shot to videotape, color-correcting it, editing it, and finally lining a master that then goes to MTV, BET, FUSE, or wherever the label needs it to be sent."

The work of music video directors and producers can be glamorous and prestigious. But directors and producers work under great stress, meeting deadlines, staying within budgets, and resolving problems among staff members. "Nine-to-five" definitely does not describe a day in the life of a music video director or producer; 16-hour days (and more) are not uncommon. Nonetheless, those able to make it in the industry find their work to be extremely enjoyable and satisfying.

Music video directors and producers frequently travel to meetings with potential employers and to filming locations. Music videos are made in almost every setting imaginable—from a dark, dingy warehouse to a Caribbean beach to a nondescript sidewalk in a small town. Successful directors and producers enjoy traveling and the demanding aspects of work in this field. Catherine often shoots in Los Angeles, but has also worked in England, Brazil, Italy, Mexico, Prague, and other countries. "Sometimes we write specifically for locations," she says, "so I do travel a lot and see parts of the world I'd never normally see."

DO I HAVE WHAT IT TAKES TO BE A MUSIC VIDEO DIRECTOR OR PRODUCER?

Music video directors must have a strong creative vision for their projects, but they must be able to work with producers, editors, record company executives, and other industry professionals. They should be decisive leaders with an excellent knowledge of music videos and the narrative forms necessary to create them.

Music video producers come from a wide variety of backgrounds. Some start out as directors, musicians, business school graduates, actors, or production assistants. Many have never formally studied music video production or film. Most producers, however, get their positions through several years of experience in the industry, perseverance, and a keen sense for what projects will be artistically and commercially successful.

HOW DO I BECOME A MUSIC VIDEO DIRECTOR OR PRODUCER?
Education
High School

The career paths of music video directors and producers are rather nontraditional. There is no standard training or normal progression up an industry ladder leading

A Short History of Music Videos

Music videos gained popular, mainstream appeal when MTV, the first all-music cable channel, was formed in 1981. But music videos have actually been around more than 100 years. In 1890, George Thomas, a photographer, created the first live-model illustrated song. Set to the song, "The Little Lost Child," this series of photographic images printed on glass slides (and backed by live singers and musicians) hit vaudeville stages, and later, movie theaters. Customers lined up to see the shows. Suddenly, a new music sub-industry was born: illustrating popular songs to help sell sheet music.

The first music videos, called Soundies, were developed in the 1940s. They were composed of footage of a band or a solo singer simply performing a song on a stage. Soundies were used to promote artists (usually jazz musicians, but also torch singers, dancers, and comedians) as videos are used today.

Richard Lester is considered to be the father of contemporary music video. His exuberant, full-length films in the mid-1960s with The Beatles, such as *A Hard Day's Night* and *Help!,* were groundbreaking explorations of music and storytelling. Many of the musical segments in these movies were precursors to styles that we see in today's music videos. In fact, MTV took notice of Lester's work by presenting him with an award for his contributions to the art of music video in the 1980s.

Michael Nesmith, a member of the rock group The Monkees, is largely credited with creating the first music videos of the modern era. He made short, musical films for the television show *Saturday Night Live* in 1979, and the first video album, *Elephant Parts,* in 1981. The art form grew quickly in the 1980s with the popularity of MTV, which played music videos 24 hours a day, seven days a week. (Today, ironically, reality television shows and other non-music programming compete with music videos for airtime on MTV.) Most recording artists released music videos for their singles to generate interest in and sales for their latest albums.

The music video industry has come a long way from George Thomas's live-model illustrated songs. Advances such as computer-generated animation, digital filming, and digital sound have given music video directors more tools to work with and the ability to produce an increasing variety of looks, sounds, and characters in their finished videos. One constant remains from Thomas's days: music videos still play a major role in helping companies sell product—whether sheet music, CDs, music videos, Internet downloads, or concert tickets.

to the jobs of director or producer. At the very least, a high school diploma, while not technically required, will still probably be indispensable to you in terms of the background and education it signifies. (A high school diploma will be necessary if you decide to attend film school.) As is true of all artists, especially those in a medium as widely disseminated as music videos, you will need to have rich and varied experience in order to create works that are intelligently crafted and speak to people of many different backgrounds.

In high school, courses in music, English (especially writing), art, theater, and history will give you a good foundation. If your high school offers film history or film production classes, be sure to take those courses. Visit the Web site of the American Film Institute (http://www.afi.edu) for a list of high schools that offer film courses and other resources for students and teachers. Don't forget to take computer classes, since computer technology plays a major role in this industry. Finally, be active in school and community drama productions, whether as a performer, set designer, or cue-card holder.

High school courses that will be of assistance to you in your work as a producer include business, mathematics, English, speech, computer science, economics, music, and psychology. Catherine advises high school students who aspire to careers as music video producers to "start at the bottom and learn everything you can. This only helps you be the ultimate problem-solver, which I feel is a huge part of my job description. If you jump in too fast without enough experience, you'll find yourself stumped when presented with issues of a great variety, such as a disgruntled crew, teamsters threatening to strike your set, and a director who wants more time than you have budgeted."

Postsecondary Training

There are more than 500 film studies programs in the United States. According to the American Film Institute, the most

reputable are Columbia University in New York City, New York University, the University of California at Los Angeles, and the University of Southern California.

The Film Institute of Technology in Los Angeles, California, offers a six-month, for-credit program that teaches students how to direct music video and commercial productions. Visit http://www.mi.edu/programs/fit.htm for more information.

The debate continues on what is more influential in a music video directing career: personal experience or professional training. Some say that it is possible for creative people to land directing jobs without having gone through a formal program. Competition is so pervasive in the industry that even film school graduates find jobs scarce (only 5 to 10 percent of the 26,000 students who graduate from film schools each year find jobs in the industry). On the other hand, film school offers an education in fundamental directing skills by working with student productions. Such education is rigorous, but in addition to teaching skills, it provides aspiring music video directors with peer groups and a network of contacts with students, faculty, and guest speakers that can be of help after graduation.

As with the career of director, a college degree is not required to be successful as a producer, but many producers earn college degrees. Formal study of business, film, television, music, communications, theater, writing, English literature, or art at the college level is helpful, as the music video producer must have a

How to Break Into the Industry

Becoming a music director or producer is not just something you can do straight out of college or with a few self-directed or -produced music videos on your resume. It takes considerable experience and a lot of grunt work to work your way up to the top levels of the music video industry. There are, however, many things you can do to break into the industry.

First of all, you need to be willing to work for little or no money to get your foot in the door. To get started, ask local bands if you can direct their next video or see if you can do the same for your church choir or another local musical group. In short, grab any directing or producing opportunity that comes along, whether it relates to music or not.

Once you have gained some experience shooting or producing music videos, you should create a demo reel of your best work and send it to record companies and other potential employers. This will show employers that you are interested in and skilled enough to enter the industry.

As mentioned earlier, film school is a breeding ground for making contacts in the industry. Often, contacts are the essential factor in getting a job; many music video industry insiders agree that it's not only what you know but who you know that will get you a job. Networking often leads to good opportunities at various types of jobs in the industry. Many professionals recommend that those who want to become directors and producers should go to Los Angeles or New York, find any industry-related job, continue to take classes, and keep their eyes and ears open for news of job openings, especially with those professionals who are admired for their talent.

Another way to start out is through the Assistant Directors Training Program of the Directors Guild of America (http://www.dga.org). This program provides an excellent opportunity to those without industry connections to work on film and television productions. The program is based at two locations, New York City for the East Coast Program and Sherman Oaks, California, for the West Coast Program. Trainees receive hands-on experience through placement with major studios or on television movies and series. Programs also include formal training through mandatory seminars.

varied knowledge base to do his or her job successfully.

Internships and Volunteerships

Many in the industry suggest that aspiring directors and producers should try to land an internship or entry-level employment as a production assistant at a production company. In addition to your regular duties, you will learn how to bid on projects, get experience writing treatments, and learn production and business tips from directors and producers.

One of the best ways to get experience is to volunteer for a student or low-budget film project; positions on such projects are often advertised in local trade publications. Community cable stations also hire volunteers and may even offer internships.

Labor Unions

Some music video directors are members of the Directors Guild of America, a union that usually negotiates salaries (as well as hours of work and other employment conditions) on behalf of its members. Others are members of the Music Video Production Company, which represents the professional interests of music video directors and producers.

WHO WILL HIRE ME?

Music video directors and producers are usually employed on a freelance or contractual basis. Directors and producers find work, for example, with record companies, with advertising agencies, and through the creation of their own independent video projects. Keep in mind that the music video industry is not the only avenue for employment. Directors and producers work on documentaries, on television productions, in the film industry, and with various types of video presentations, from music to business. The greatest concentrations of music video directors and producers are in Los Angeles and New York City. Nearly 37,000 directors and producers are employed in the television, video, cable, and motion picture industries.

Rarely do people start their careers as music video directors or producers. People usually work their way up into these positions by starting in entry-level jobs in the industry. After college, Catherine moved to Los Angeles without knowing a soul. She answered ads in trade magazines and finally landed a job at a commercial production company as an in-house editor. "There," she recalls, "I met lots of people and finally decided to go freelance into production to start on the path I really wanted, which was to end up producing. I worked my way up the ranks. I did everything, production assisting, video assisting, assistant stylist, craft services, and finally got the opportunity to work in the production office. And there I stayed working as a production coordinator, then a production manager, and I got my first break when the producer I was working with on a huge Toyota commercial campaign quit. The director, whom I had been working with for a while, came to me, and said, 'You're ready. I want you to produce this.' I did, and became his regular producer. From then on, I freelanced at different companies as a producer until one company liked me enough to ask me to stay and be on staff as its head of production. And after a time, I was promoted to executive producer."

WHERE CAN I GO FROM HERE?

In the music video industry, advancement often comes with recognition. Directors who work on well-received music videos receive awards as well as more lucrative and prestigious job offers. Some directors choose to advance by leaving the music video industry for work in the motion picture industry or other related industries. Spike Jonze is an excellent example of a music video director who made the jump to feature-film directing. In the early 1990s, Jonze made a name for himself as the director of well-received music videos for REM and the Beastie Boys, and then used the skills he developed directing music videos to create award-winning feature films such as *Being John Malkovich* and *Adaptation.* Other music video directors who have made the transition to feature film directing include Brett Ratner (*Rush Hour, Red Dragon*), David Fincher (*Fight Club, Panic Room*), and Michael Bay (*Armageddon, Pearl Harbor*).

Advancement for producers is generally measured by the types of projects they do, increased earnings, and respect in the field. Some producers become directors or make enough money to finance their own projects. Catherine hopes to one day produce a major feature film.

WHAT ARE THE SALARY RANGES?

According to the *Music Video Insider,* music video directors earn approximately 10 percent of a video's operating budget before production fees and insurance costs are factored into the budget. Budgets can range from as little as a few thousand dollars to millions of dollars for the creation of a video for a top artist. The U.S. Department of Labor reports that the median annual salary for direc-

> ### Related Jobs
>
> - actors
> - art directors
> - camera operators
> - cinematographers and directors of photography
> - film and television editors
> - film and television extras
> - music producers
> - music video editors
> - musicians
> - pop/rock musicians
> - producers
> - screenwriters

tors and producers employed in the video and motion picture industries was $89,410 in 2004. Some directors and producers earned as little as $26,940 a year, while those with years of experience and solid reputations in the business can earn upwards of $120,000. Directors and producers who work on a freelance basis must pay for their own health insurance as well as the costs of operating a business.

WHAT IS THE JOB OUTLOOK?

According to the U.S. Department of Labor, employment for directors and producers is expected to grow about as fast as the average for all occupations through 2014. Though opportunities will increase with the expansion of cable and satellite television and an increased overseas demand for American-made music videos and films, competition is extreme and turnover is high. Most positions in the music video industry are held on a freelance basis. As is the case with most careers in the music video industry, directors and producers are usually hired to work on one video at a time. After a video is completed, new contacts must be made for further assignments.

Music Writers and Editors

SUMMARY

Definition
Music writers express, edit, promote, and interpret ideas and facts in written form for books, magazines, trade journals, and newspapers. Music editors perform a wide range of functions, but their primary responsibility is to ensure that text provided by music writers is suitable for the intended audiences.

Alternative Job Titles
Music critics
Music journalists

Salary Range
$24,320 to $46,420 to
 $89,940+ (music writers)
$20,000 to $45,510 to
 $85,230+ (music editors)

Educational Requirements
Bachelor's degree

Certification or Licensing
None available

Employment Outlook
About as fast as the average

High School Subjects
English (writing/literature)
Journalism
Music

Personal Interests
Music
Reading/Books
Writing

"As a critic," says Greg Kot, a music writer in Chicago, "it is important to realize that you are not operating in a vacuum. You are part of a community, for better or worse. This means not just writing about music, but meeting the bands, artists, and fans that your writing sometimes may rub the wrong way. So I've had a beer poured on me at a bar by a musician who was upset with something I wrote about him. Once a fan threw a piece of sod at me during an outdoor concert and hit me in the side of the head. I also got into a scuffle with a fan at a rock concert. The bouncer at the show came by just in time to break up the fight, and probably saved me from getting a broken nose. The bottom line: Make sure you believe in everything you write. Some day you may have to defend yourself for writing it."

WHAT DO MUSIC WRITERS AND EDITORS DO?

Music writers write about new releases and recent performances by all types of musicians. They research artists or bands, watch or listen to them perform, and then write a review or story. Some music writers also write columns for newspaper or magazine publication or commentary for radio or television broadcast.

Music writers conduct their research by attending musical shows or listening to compact discs, music downloads, or music in other formats. If they are reviewing a live performance, they may take notes detailing the concert's venue, crowd, atmosphere, and other factors that will make their review more interesting and thorough.

Though some music writers may simply report objectively on music news, most write criticism. To garner respect and credibility, their opinions on performances or recordings must be fair, but honest. To do this, music writers compare the performance or album release with previous works of the artist or band in question and also compare it with other similar music artists. For example, if a writer is reviewing a young pop star's latest CD, he or she would not compare it to the work of a classical orchestra, but perhaps might hold it up to the work of rock stars from previous eras, such as the Beatles, Elvis Presley, or the Rolling Stones.

Music journalists write more than just reviews. They also write personal articles about artists and bands. These stories may originate as an assignment from a music editor or as the result of a lead or news tip. Good music writers are always on the lookout for new story ideas.

To write a personal music article, music writers gather and verify facts by interviewing the artist or band and also talk to people involved in the production or organization of a music show or recording. During interviews, writers generally take notes or use a tape recorder to collect information and write the story once back in their office. When under tight deadline, music writers might have little time between their last interview and publication, and may enlist the help of editors and other writers to review and help organize their material. Together, they will decide what emphasis, or angle, to give the story and make sure it is written to meet prescribed standards of editorial style and format.

Music editors work with music writers on the staffs of newspapers, magazines, publishing houses, and other organizations that employ writers. Their primary responsibility is to make sure that text provided by music writers is suitable in content, format, and style for the intended audiences. A music editor working for a newspaper, for instance, would ensure that articles are timely and can be understood and enjoyed by the newspaper's average reader—not just people in the music industry.

Editors must make sure that all text to be printed or placed on Web sites is well written, factually correct (sometimes this job is done by a *researcher* or *fact checker*), and grammatically correct. Other editors, including managing editors, editors-in-chief, and editorial directors, have managerial responsibilities and work with heads of other departments, such as marketing, sales, and production.

Music writers and editors are employed either as in-house staff or as freelancers. Pay varies according to experience and the position, but freelancers must provide their own office space and equipment

To Be a Successful Music Writer, You Should . . .

- have a good knowledge of many musical genres

- have strong writing skills

- be assertive and tenacious when interviewing sometimes uncooperative musicians

- have strong communication skills

- be willing to work odd or long hours to cover concerts and other events

- be able to work under deadline pressure

such as computers, phones, and fax machines. Freelance writers and editors are also responsible for attracting clients, keeping tax records, sending out invoices, negotiating contracts, and providing their own health insurance.

WHAT IS IT LIKE TO BE A MUSIC WRITER OR EDITOR?

Greg Kot has worked as a music critic at the *Chicago Tribune* since 1990. He also is the cohost (with Jim DeRogatis) of "Sound Opinions," the world's only rock and roll talk show (visit http://soundop-inions.com to learn more about the show). Greg has written for numerous magazines, including *Rolling Stone, Blender,*

and *Entertainment Weekly,* and is the author of *Wilco: Learning How to Die* (New York: Random House, 2004). "I wanted to be a writer and a journalist, first and foremost," Greg recalls. "I wanted to work at a newspaper in Chicago, and I'd been reading the *Tribune* since I was a kid. Music criticism was something I did in my spare time. I loved writing and I loved music, so combining the two seemed natural. For years I wrote my own music fanzine and published it myself, with the help of friends, even while working as an editor at the *Tribune.* I never expected that I would get paid for writing music criticism. While still working as an editor, I started covering concerts for the *Tribune,* mainly because no one else was writing about the concerts I wanted to see. Eventually I was offered the critic's job when the previous critic retired."

To Be a Successful Music Editor, You Should . . .

- have a keen eye for detail

- have good information management skills

- have a good knowledge of many musical genres

- be able to wok well with others

- be able to work under deadline pressure

One of the most challenging aspects of a music critic's job are the long and unconventional hours. "I cover concerts at night," says Greg, "so my day usually begins at 10 A.M., and sometimes doesn't end until 1 or 2 A.M. the next morning. I usually work 55 to 60 hours a week, and rarely get a full day off, because many concerts I need to cover are on weekends. In the morning, I will make a few phone calls and trade e-mails with record company publicists to set up interviews or to request information about artists I am covering. I will spend most of the day conducting interviews, either on the phone or in person, and writing articles. I write four to eight articles a week of varying length, including concert reviews, album reviews, profiles, trend pieces, and my weekly column."

DO I HAVE WHAT IT TAKES TO BE A MUSIC WRITER OR EDITOR?

Good music editors and writers are analytical people who know how to think clearly and communicate what they are thinking. They must also be aggressive, persistent, detail-oriented, and inquisitive. "You must be scrupulous about facts, dates, and names," Greg recommends. "You must be reliable: Turn in clean copy, and turn it in on time. Beyond those basics, your greatest asset as a writer and journalist is your curiosity. You must always want to know more."

Music writers should enjoy interaction with people of various races, cultures, religions, economic levels, and social sta-

---

Music Magazines on the Web

Billboard
http://www.billboard.com

Blender
http://www.blender.com/in_print

CMJ New Music Monthly
http://www.cmj.com

Dirty Linen
http://www.dirtylinen.com

Downbeat
http://www.downbeat.com

International Musician
http://www.afm.org/public/home/index.php

Q
http://www.q4music.com

Rolling Stone
http://www.rollingstone.com

Spin
http://www.spin.com

Vibe
http://www.vibe.com

---

tuses. For some jobs—on a newspaper, for example, where the activity is hectic and deadlines are short—the ability to concentrate and produce under pressure is essential. Although not essential, knowledge of shorthand or speedwriting makes note-taking easier, and an acquaintance with photography is an asset.

Music criticism is a highly specialized field, one that blends music knowledge and expressive writing skills. The glamour of attending concerts and meeting musicians is an undeniable benefit. However, this job also includes possible stress and irregular hours. To succeed as a writer, you have to have passion about the subject in which you write. "You need passion for your job, for the craft of writing, for the ethics and integrity of journalism," Greg explains. "This is a noble profession. Journalists can change the world through what they write. In a sense, they are writing the first draft of today's history as it is being made. It is a huge responsibility and a privilege."

You should also be able to appreciate (if not *like*) all forms of music and have in-depth knowledge of the evolution of music trends, scenes, and sounds to place artists in their historical context.

HOW DO I BECOME A MUSIC WRITER OR EDITOR?

Education

High School

High school courses that will provide you with a firm foundation for a music writing and/or editing career include English, journalism, music history, band, communications, typing, and computer science. Speech courses will help you hone your interviewing skills, which are necessary for success as a writer. In addition, it will be helpful to take college prep courses, such as foreign language, history, math, and science.

Postsecondary Training

Most newspapers, magazines, and other employers of music writers and editors seek candidates with at least a bachelor's degree, and a graduate degree will give you an advantage when applying for positions.

Many music writers have backgrounds in general journalism. More than 400 colleges offer bachelor's degrees in journalism. In these schools, approximately three-fourths of a student's time is devoted to a liberal arts education and one-fourth to the professional study of journalism, with required courses such as introductory mass media, basic reporting and copy editing, history of journalism, and press law and ethics. Students are encouraged to select other journalism courses according to their specific interests (in this case, music classes). Greg studied journalism in college, and also worked for the student newspaper. "Both experiences proved quite valuable," he says.

Other music writers and editors get their educational background in music. They may major in music theory, criticism, or performance and develop their writing skills by minoring in journalism or simply through reporting experience.

In addition to formal course work, most employers look for practical writing and editing experience. If you have worked on high school or college newspapers, yearbooks, or literary magazines, you will make a better candidate, as well as if you have worked for small community newspapers or radio stations, even in unpaid positions.

Internships and Volunteerships

Many book publishers, magazines, newspapers, and radio and television stations have summer internship programs that provide valuable training if you want to learn about the publishing and broadcasting businesses. Interns do many simple tasks, such as running errands and answering phones, but some may be asked to perform research, conduct interviews, or even write some minor pieces. Greg participated in several summer internships with small daily newspapers. He says the internships expanded his knowledge and prepared him well for working at a daily newspaper.

You can explore a career as a music writer in a number of ways. Talk to reporters and editors at local newspapers and radio and TV stations. Interview the admissions counselor at the school of journalism closest to your home to get a sense of the type of students who apply and are accepted into journalism programs.

You should also read the work of music writers to get a sense of how they organize and structure their reviews and articles. Take note of when a music critic writes a particularly positive or negative review and how he or she handles writing it honestly but tactfully. See page 98 for Web sites of popular music magazines that publish excerpts of reviews online.

In addition to taking courses in English, journalism, music, speech, computer science, and typing, high school students can acquire practical experience by working on school newspapers or a community organization's newsletter. Part-time and summer jobs with newspapers or radio stations provide invaluable experience to the aspiring music reporter.

WHO WILL HIRE ME?

Music writers and editors are employed by newspapers, magazines, wire services, and radio and television broadcasting companies. They may write for general news periodicals that have entertainment sections or for specialty music magazines, such as *Rolling Stone* or *Blender*. Some work as staff writers, but many are freelancers and write for several publications.

A fair amount of experience is required before you can call yourself a music writer or editor. Most people start out in entry-level positions, such as junior writer, copy editor, or researcher. These jobs may be listed with college career services offices or they can be obtained by applying directly to individual publishers or broadcasting companies. Graduates who previously held internships at newspapers, radio stations, or related employers often have the advantage of knowing someone who can give them a personal recommendation and leads on jobs. Want ads in newspapers and trade journals are another source for jobs.

After graduating from college, Greg was hired at the *Quad-City Times* in Davenport, Iowa, and then soon after by the *Chicago Tribune*. "At both papers," he says, "I did many jobs, and learned a number of skills—police-beat reporting, city government reporting, page design, photography, even editing—before eventually landing the job I'm in now as a music critic. It's rare to get a full-time gig at a big daily newspaper as a rock critic. I didn't think it was possible. But I learned how to be a journalist first, and the skills I learned along the way led to the job I have now."

WHERE CAN I GO FROM HERE?

Employees who start as editorial assistants and show promise may be given a wider range of duties while retaining the same title. Eventually they may become editors or staff writers. They may progress from less significant stories and tasks to important music news and feature stories. As they accrue experience, they may be promoted to other editorial or writing positions that come with greater responsibility and pay. They may also choose to pursue managerial positions within the field of music editing and writing, such as *managing editor* and *editor-in-chief.* These positions involve more management and decision making than is usually found in the positions described previously. The editor-in-chief works with the publisher to ensure that a suitable editorial policy is being followed, while the managing editor is responsible for all aspects of the editorial department.

As is the case within many editorial and writing positions, a music writer or editor may advance by moving from a position on one publication or company to the same position with a larger or more prestigious publication or company. Such moves may involve an increase in both salary and prestige.

Freelance or self-employed writers earn advancement in the form of larger fees as they gain exposure and establish their reputations as music critics and writers.

WHAT ARE THE SALARY RANGES?

There are great variations in the earnings of music writers and editors. Salaries are related to experience, the type and size of media outlet for which the writer or editor works, and geographic location.

In 2005, median annual earnings for salaried writers and authors were $46,420 a year, according to the U.S. Department of Labor. The lowest 10 percent earned less than $24,320, while the highest 10 percent earned $89,940 or more. In 2005, the mean annual earnings for writers in newspaper and book publishing were $47,950, while those employed in radio and television broadcasting earned $47,620. In addition to their salaries, many music writers earn some income from freelance work. Part-time freelancers may earn from $5,000 to $15,000 a year. Freelance earnings vary widely. Full-time established freelance writers may earn up to $75,000 a year.

The salaries of music editors are roughly comparable to those of other editors. Median annual earnings for all editors were $45,510 in 2005, according to the U.S. Department of Labor. The lowest 10 percent earned less than $26,910 and

Related Jobs

- columnists
- copywriters
- corporate writers
- essayists
- foreign correspondents
- novelists
- playwrights
- poets
- public relations specialists
- reporters
- screenwriters
- technical writers and editors

the highest 10 percent earned $85,230 or more. In 2005, the mean annual earnings for editors in newspaper and book publishing were $51,030, while those employed in radio and television broadcasting earned $47,750. Starting salaries of $20,000 or less are still common in many areas.

WHAT IS THE JOB OUTLOOK?

Employment opportunities in writing and editing are expected to increase about as fast as the average for all occupations through 2014, according to the U.S. Department of Labor. Because of the narrow scope of music writing and editing, however, competition for jobs will be very intense. Individuals with previous experience and specialized education in music and reporting will be the most successful at finding jobs.

The demand for music writers and editors will be higher in big cities such as New York, Chicago, and Seattle, because of their large and busy music scenes. But those just breaking into journalism might find better luck starting at smaller community newspapers and other publications. In general, opportunities will be best for writers and editors who are willing to relocate and accept relatively low starting salaries.

Strong employment growth is expected for music writers and editors who are employed by online newspapers and magazines.

Singers and Songwriters

SUMMARY

Definition
Singers are musicians who use their voices as their instruments, and may perform as part of a band, choir, or other musical ensembles, or solo, with or without musical accompaniment. Songwriters write the words and music for songs, including songs for recordings, advertising jingles, and theatrical performances. Many songwriters perform their own songs.

Alternative Job Titles
Musicians

Salary Range
$13,541 to $37,253 to $109,990+

Educational Requirements
High school diploma

Certification or Licensing
None available

Employment Outlook
About as fast as the average

High School Subjects
English (writing/literature)
Music
Speech
Theater

Personal Interests
Entertaining/performing
Music
Theater

Justin Roberts, a children's musician in Chicago, Illinois, says that he loves performing for families because it is such a communal event. "Seeing parents and even grandparents with their kids smiling and singing along never gets old," he says. "And getting to witness the unabashed joy of kids just breaking into song or spontaneously starting a kiddie mosh pit is a delight. I love my job. Of course, there is a lot of hard work involved in making a living as a musician as well, but it's all worth it."

WHAT DO SINGERS AND SONGWRITERS DO?

Essentially, *singers* are employed to perform music with their voices by using their knowledge of vocal sound and delivery, harmony, melody, and rhythm. They put their individual vocal styles into the songs they sing, and they interpret music accordingly. The inherent sounds of the voices in a performance play a significant part in how a song will affect an audience; this essential aspect of a singer's voice is known as its tone. The following paragraphs provide an overview of the many types of singers.

Classical singers are usually categorized according to the range and quality of their voices, beginning with the highest singing voice, the soprano, and ending with the lowest, the bass; voices in between include mezzo-soprano, contralto, tenor, and baritone. Singers perform either alone (in which case they are referred to as soloists) or as members of an ensemble, or group. They sing by either following a score, which is the printed musical text, or by memorizing the material. Also, they may sing either with or without instrumental accompaniment; singing without accompaniment is called a cappella. In opera—actually plays set to music—singers perform the various roles, much as actors, interpreting the drama with their voice to the accompaniment of a symphony orchestra.

Classical singers may perform a variety of musical styles, or specialize in a specific period; they may give recitals, or perform as members of an ensemble. Classical singers generally undergo years of voice training and instruction in musical theory. They develop their vocal technique and learn how to project without harming their voices. Classical singers rarely use a microphone when they sing; nonetheless, their voices must be heard above the orchestra. Because classical singers often perform music from many different languages, they learn how to pronounce these languages, and often how to speak them as well. Those who are involved in opera work for opera companies in major cities throughout the country and often travel extensively. Some classical singers also perform in other musical areas.

Professional singers tend to perform in a certain chosen style of music, such as jazz, rock, or blues, among many others. Many singers pursue careers that will lead them to perform for coveted recording contracts, on concert tours, and for television and motion pictures. Others perform in rock, pop, country, gospel, or folk groups, singing in concert halls, nightclubs, and churches, and at social gatherings and for small studio recordings. Virtuosos, classical artists who are expertly skilled in their singing style, tend to perform traditional pieces that have been handed down through hundreds of years. Singers in other areas often perform popular, current pieces, and often songs that they themselves have composed.

Another style of music in which formal training is often helpful is jazz. *Jazz singers* learn phrasing, breathing, and vocal techniques; often, the goal of a jazz singer is to become as much a part of the instrumentation as the piano, saxophone, trumpet, or trombone. Many jazz singers perform "scat" singing, in which the voice is used in an improvisational way much like any other instrument.

Folk singers perform songs that may be many years old, or they may write their own songs. Folk singers generally perform songs that express a certain cultural tradition; while some folk singers specialize in their own or another culture, others may sing songs from a great variety of cultural and musical traditions. In the United States, folk singing is particularly linked to the acoustic guitar, and many singers accompany themselves with one while singing.

A cappella singing, which is singing without musical accompaniment, takes many forms. A cappella music may be a part of classical music; it may also be a part of folk music, as in the singing of barbershop quartets. Another form, called doo-wop, is closely linked to rock and rhythm and blues music.

Gospel music, which evolved in the United States, is a form of sacred music; *gospel singers* generally sing as part of a choir, accompanied by an organ, or other musical instruments, but may also perform a cappella. Many popular singers began their careers as singers in church and gospel choirs before entering jazz, pop, blues, or rock.

Pop/rock singers generally require no formal training whatsoever. Rock music is a very broad term encompassing many different styles of music, such as heavy metal, punk, rap, rhythm and blues, rockabilly, techno, and many others. Many popular rock singers cannot even sing. But rock singers learn to express themselves and their music, developing their own phrasing and vocal techniques. Rock singers usually sing as part of a band, or with a backing band to accompany them. Rock singers usually sing with microphones so that they can be heard above the amplified instruments around them.

All singers practice and rehearse their songs and music. Some singers read from music scores while performing; others perform from memory. Yet all must gain an intimate knowledge of their music so that they can best convey its meanings and feelings to their audience. Singers must also exercise their voices even when not performing. Some singers perform as featured soloists and artists. Others perform as part of a choir, or as backup singers adding harmony to the lead singer's voice.

Some singers write their own songs, while others seek out *songwriters* to help them create material that works with their vocal style and talents. There are many different ways to write a song. A song may begin with a few words (the lyric) or with a few notes of a melody, or a song may be suggested by an idea, theme, or product. A song may come about in a flash of inspiration or may be developed slowly over a long period of time. Songwriters may work alone, or as part of a team, in which one person concentrates on the lyrics while another person concentrates on the music. Sometimes there may be several people working on the same song.

Most popular songs require words, or lyrics, and some songwriters may concentrate on writing the words to a song. These songwriters are called *lyricists.* Events, experiences, or emotions may inspire a lyricist to write lyrics. A lyricist may also be contracted to write the words for a jingle or musical, or to adapt the words from an existing song for another project.

Some songwriters do no more than write the words to a potential song, and leave it to others to develop a melody and musical accompaniment for the words. They may sell the words to a music publisher, or work in a team to create a finished song from the lyric. Some lyricists specialize in writing the words for advertising jingles. They are usually employed by advertising agencies and may work on several different products at once, often under pressure of a deadline.

In songwriting teams, one member may be a lyricist, while the other member is a *composer*. The development of a song can be a highly collaborative process. The composer might suggest topics for the song to the lyricist; the lyricist might suggest a melody to the composer. Other times, the composer plays a musical piece for the lyricist, and the lyricist tries to create lyrics to fit with that piece.

Composers for popular music generally have a strong background in music, and often in performing music as well. They must have an understanding of many musical styles so that they can develop the music that will fit a project's needs. Composers work with a variety of musical and electronic equipment, including computers, to produce and record their music. They develop the different parts for the different musical instruments needed to play the song. They also work with musicians who will play and record the song, and the composer conducts or otherwise directs the musicians as the song is played.

Songwriters, composers, and musicians often make use of MIDI (musical instrument digital interface) technology to produce sounds through synthesizers, drum machines, and samplers. These sounds are usually controlled by a computer, and the composer or songwriter can mix, alter, and refine the sounds using mixing boards and computer software. Like analog or acoustic instruments, which produce sounds as a string or reed or drum head vibrates with air, MIDI creates digital "vibrations" that can produce sounds similar to acoustic instruments or highly unusual sounds invented by the songwriter. Synthesizers and other sound-producing machines may each have their own keyboard or playing mechanism, or be linked through one or more keyboards. They may also be controlled through the computer, or with other types of controls, such as a guitar controller, which plays like a guitar, or foot controls. Songs can be stored in the computer, or transferred to tape or compact disc.

For most songwriters, writing a song is only the first part of their job. After a song is written, songwriters usually produce a "demo" of the song, so that the client or potential purchaser of the song can hear how it sounds. Songwriters contract with recording studios, studio musicians, and recording engineers to produce a version of the song. The songwriter then submits the song to a publishing house, record company, recording artist, film studio, or others, who will then decide if the song is appropriate for their needs. Often, a songwriter will produce several versions of a song, or submit several different songs for a particular project. There is always a chance that one, some, or all of them will sell.

WHAT IS IT LIKE TO BE A SINGER OR SONGWRITER?

Justin Roberts is a Chicago-based singer/songwriter who specializes in children's music.

He has released five CDs for children, three of which have won Parents' Choice Gold Awards. *Child Magazine* and Amazon.com also named one of these recordings, *Way Out*, one of the 10 best children's CDs of the year. (Visit http://www.justinroberts.org to learn more about Justin and to hear samples of his music.)

Justin began performing music at a young age, participating in youth choirs and local theater. In high school, he formed an original rock band, and in college was a principal player in the alternative folk group Pimentos for Gus. "While performing with Pimentos in Minneapolis, I made my living as a preschool teacher," Justin recalls. "I began writing songs for the kids at my school, and some of these songs ended up on my debut CD for children, *Great Big Sun* (which was recorded in 1997). I had no plans to be a

To Be a Successful Songwriter, You Should . . .

- be creative and imaginative
- be familiar with a variety of musical styles
- have a working knowledge of musical instruments, especially the piano
- be able to invent melodies and combine melodies into a song
- have a love of language and music
- be willing to receive constructive criticism regarding your talents
- have strong ambition and be dedicated to achieving success in the field
- have technical knowledge regarding the latest in modern recording techniques

To Be a Successful Singer, You Should . . .

- have an inborn love and talent for singing
- know how to read and write music
- learn to use your voice in a way that provides good expression to your songs, music, and ideas
- be willing to receive constructive criticism regarding your talents
- have strong ambition and be dedicated to achieving success in the field

children's performer at the time, I just found myself writing the songs." After the breakup of his band, Justin began releasing more CDs for kids. Today, he performs all over the country and owns his own record label, Carpet Square Records.

Justin spends about 75 percent of his time running his record label (manufacturing CDs, dealing with distributers, publicists, booking agents, planning his performances, etc.) and the remainder of the time performing, writing songs, and recording new material. "I perform nationwide in small and large theaters, rock clubs, festivals, and some non-traditional venues," he says. "I am on the road nearly every weekend and often during the week as well. I perform more than 200 shows a year. About every one-and-a-half years, I release a new CD. I will often take a brief break from performing to concentrate on finishing songs for a new record and planning the recording with my producer, Liam Davis."

DO I HAVE WHAT IT TAKES TO BE A SINGER OR SONGWRITER?

Learning to sing and becoming a singer is often a matter of desire, practice, and an inborn love and talent for singing. Learning to play a musical instrument is often extremely helpful in learning to sing and to read and write music. Sometimes it is not even necessary to have a "good" singing voice. Many singers in rock music have less-than-perfect voices, and rap artists do not really sing at all. But these singers learn to use their voices in ways that nonetheless provide good expression to their songs, music, and ideas.

Many elements of songwriting cannot really be learned but are a matter of inborn talent. A creative imagination and the ability to invent melodies and combine melodies into a song are essential parts of a songwriting career. As you become more familiar with your own talents, and with songwriting, you'll learn to develop and enhance your creative skills. "While writing songs for kids," Justin says, "I try to please myself first and foremost. I don't

think about writing for kids as much as about writing a good song. I do the same things I would do when writing a song for adults—try to create a good melody with some hooks and well-crafted lyrics."

In order to continue to grow with the music industry, singers and songwriters must be tuned into new musical styles and trends. They must also keep up with developments in music technology. A great deal of time is spent making and maintaining contacts with others in the music industry.

HOW DO I BECOME A SINGER OR SONGWRITER?
Education

"I didn't really train for this career," says Justin, "I just followed my passions. I have always loved music and spent much of my free time listening to music or playing it when I was young. I was not really interested in studying music in school, though I did take a few music courses." Justin majored in philosophy of religion at Kenyon College in Ohio. "While I was there," he recalls, "I played in a band and sang in an all-male a capella group called the Kokosingers, with Liam Davis (who later became my producer, arranger, and multi-instrumentalist). Following college, I moved to Minneapolis, Minnesota, to perform with my alternative folk band Pimentos for Gus. When Pimentos broke up, I returned to studying religion at the University of Chicago, where I received an M.A. in Divinity. During these years, I was writing songs for kids, and in 2001 (when I released *Yellow Bus*) decided to pursue it full time."

High School

Many singers require no formal training in order to sing; however, those interested in becoming classical or jazz singers should begin learning and honing their talent when they are quite young. Vocal talent can be recognized in grade school students and even in younger children. In general, these early years are a time of vast development and growth in singing ability. Evident changes occur in boys' and girls' voices when they are around 12 to 14 years old, during which time their vocal cords go through a process of lengthening and thickening. Boys' voices tend to change much more so than girls' voices, although both genders should be provided with challenges that will help them achieve their talent goals. Young students should learn about breath control and why it is necessary; they should learn to follow a conductor, including the relationship between hand and baton motions and the dynamics of the music; and they should learn about musical concepts such as tone, melody, harmony, and rhythm.

During the last two years of high school, aspiring singers should have a good idea of what classification they are in, according to the range and quality of their voices: soprano, alto, contralto, tenor, baritone, or bass. These categories indicate the resonance of the voice—soprano being the highest and lightest, bass being the lowest and heaviest. Students should take part in voice classes, choirs, and ensembles. In addition, students should continue their studies in English, writing, social studies, foreign language, and other electives in music, theory, and performance.

There tend to be no formal educational requirements for those who wish to be singers. Formal education is valuable, though, especially in younger years. Some students know early in their lives that they want to be singers and are ambitious enough to continue to practice and learn. These students are often advised to attend high schools that are specifically geared toward combined academic and intensive arts education in music, dance, and theater. Such schools can provide valuable preparation and guidance for those who plan to pursue professional careers in the arts. Admission is usually based on results from students' auditions as well as academic testing.

If you are interested in becoming a songwriter, you should take courses in music that involve you with singing, playing instruments, and studying the history of music. Theater and speech classes will help you to understand the nature of performing, as well as involve you in writing dramatic pieces. You should study poetry in an English class, and try your hand at composing poetry in different forms. Language skills can also be honed in foreign-language classes and by working on student literary magazines. An understanding of how people act and think can influence you as a lyricist, so take courses in psychology and sociology.

Postsecondary Training

Many find it worthwhile and fascinating to continue their study of music and voice in a liberal arts program at a college or university. Similarly, others attend schools of higher education that are focused specifically on music, such as the Juilliard School (http://www.juilliard.edu) in New York. Such an intense program would include a multidisciplinary curriculum of composition and performance, as well as study and appreciation of the history, development, variety, and potential advances of music. In this type of program, a student would earn a Bachelor of Arts degree. To earn a Bachelor of Science degree in music, one would study musicology, which concerns the history, literature, and cultural background of music; the music industry, which will prepare one for not only singing but also marketing music and other business aspects; and professional performance. Specific music classes in a typical four-year liberal arts program would include such courses as introduction to music, music styles and structures, harmony, theory of music, elementary and advanced auditory training, music history, and individual instruction.

In addition to learning at schools, many singers are taught by private singing teachers and voice coaches, who help to develop and refine students' voices. Many aspiring singers take courses at adult continuing-education centers, where they can take advantage of courses in beginning and advanced singing, basic vocal techniques, voice coaching, and vocal performance workshops. When one is involved in voice training, he or she must learn about good articulation and breath control, which are very important qualities for all singers. Performers must take care of their voices and keep their lungs in good condition. Voice training, whether as part of a college curriculum or in private study, is useful to many singers, not only for classical and opera singers, but also for jazz singers and for those interested in careers in musical theater. Many professional singers who have already "made it" continue to take voice lessons throughout their careers.

There are no real requirements for entering the field of songwriting. All songwriters, however, will benefit from musical training, including musical theory and musical notation. Learning to play one or more instruments, such as the piano or guitar, will be especially useful in writing songs. Not all songwriters need to be able to sing, but this is helpful.

Songwriting is an extremely competitive field. Despite a lack of formal educational requirements, prospective songwriters are encouraged to continue their education through high school and preferably towards a college degree. Much of the musical training a songwriter needs, however, can also be learned informally. In general, you should have a background in music theory, and in arrangement and orchestration for multiple instruments. You should be able to read music, and be able to write it in the proper musical notation. You should have a good sense of the sounds each type of musical instrument produces, alone and in combination. Understanding harmony is important, as well as a proficiency in or understanding of a variety of styles of music. For example, you should know what makes rock different from reggae, blues, or jazz. Studies in music history will also help develop this understanding.

On the technical side, you should understand the various features, capabilities, and requirements of modern recording techniques. You should be familiar with MIDI and computer technology, as these play important roles in composing, playing, and recording music today.

Internships and Volunteerships

Aspiring singers do not generally participate in internships in the same manner as other students. Instead, at a very young age, they begin taking music and voice lessons; participating in school bands and choirs; and learning as much as they can about singing and music by visiting Web sites, listening to music, and talking with their teachers about the field. Many high school students form their own bands, playing rock, country, or jazz, and can gain experience performing before an audience; some of these young musicians even get paid to perform at school parties and other social functions. In college, they continue performing music, honing their talents, and learning about the field.

Aspiring songwriters gain experience in much the same way as singers—by learning about music, practicing their craft, and discussing the field with songwriters and musicians. Those who decide to pursue postsecondary music study might participate in an internship at a musical publisher; film, television, or video production studio; or advertising agency.

Labor Unions

Many singers and songwriters are members of trade unions, which represent them in matters such as wage scales and fair working conditions. Vocal performers who sing for studio recordings are represented by the American Federation of Television and Radio Artists; solo opera singers, solo concert singers, and choral singers are members of the American Guild of Musical Artists. Trade organizations that represent the professional interests of songwriters include the Songwriters Guild of America, the Nashville Songwriters Association, and the Songwriters and Lyricists Club.

WHO WILL HIRE ME?

There are many different environments in which singers can be employed, including local lounges, bars, cafes, radio and television, theater productions, cruise ships, resorts, hotels, casinos, large concert tours, and opera companies.

Many singers hire agents, who usually receive a percentage of the singer's earnings for finding them appropriate performance contracts. Others are employed primarily as studio singers, which means that they do not perform for live audiences but rather record their singing in studios for albums, radio, television, and motion pictures.

There is no single correct way of entering the singing profession. It is recommended that aspiring singers explore the avenues that interest them, continuing to apply and audition for whichever medium suits them. Singing is an extremely creative profession, and singers must learn to be creative and resourceful in the business matters of finding "gigs."

Most songwriters work freelance, competing for contracts to write songs for a particular artist, television show, video program, or for contracts with musical publishers and advertising agencies. They meet with clients to determine the nature of the project and to get an idea of what kind of music the client seeks, the budget for the project, the time in which the project is expected to be completed, and in what form the work is to be submitted. Many songwriters work under contract with one or more music publishing houses. Usually, they must fulfill a certain quota of new songs each year. These songwriters receive a salary, called an advance or draw, which is often paid by the week. Once a song has been published, the money earned by the song goes to pay back the songwriter's draw. A percentage of the money earned by the song over and above the amount of the draw goes to the songwriter as a royalty. Other songwriters are employed by so-called "jingle houses," that is, companies that supply music for advertising commercials. Whereas most songwriters work in their own homes or offices, these songwriters work at the jingle house's offices. Film, television, and video production studios may also employ songwriters on their staff.

WHERE CAN I GO FROM HERE?

In the singing profession and the music industry in general, the nature of the business is such that singers can consider themselves to have "made it" when they get steady, full-time work. A measure of advancement is how well known and respected singers become in their field, which in turn influences their earnings. In most areas, particularly classical music, only the most talented and persistent singers make it to the top of their profession. In other areas, success may be largely a matter of luck and perseverance. A singer on Broadway, for example, may begin as a member of the chorus, and eventually become a featured singer. On the other hand, those who have a certain passion for their work and accept their career position tend to enjoy working in local performance centers, nightclubs, and other musical environments.

Also, many experienced singers who have had formal training will become voice teachers. Reputable schools such as Juilliard consider it a plus when a student can say that he or she has studied with a master.

It is important for a songwriter to develop a strong portfolio of work and a reputation for professionalism. Songwriters who establish a reputation for producing quality work will receive larger and higher-paying projects as their careers progress. They may be contracted to score major motion pictures, or to write songs for major recording artists. Ultimately, they may be able to support themselves on their songwriting alone and also have the ability to pick and choose the projects they will work on.

Songwriters specializing in jingles and other commercial products may eventually start up their own jingle house. Other songwriters, especially those who have written a number of hit songs, may themselves become recording artists.

Over the past several years, Justin has stayed extremely busy writing and performing music and running his record company. "I love what I do," he says. "I'd like to continue performing for families nationwide, releasing records, and producing videos and DVDs."

WHAT ARE THE SALARY RANGES?

As with many occupations in the performing arts, earnings for singers are highly dependent on one's professional reputation and thus cover a wide range. To some degree, pay is also related to educational background (as it relates to how well one has been trained) and geographic location of performances. In certain situations, such as singing for audio recordings, pay is dependent on the number of minutes of finished music; for instance, an hour's pay will be given for each three-and-a-half minutes of recorded song.

Singing is often considered a glamorous occupation, but because it attracts so many professionals, competition for positions is very high. Only a small proportion of those who aspire to be singers achieve glamorous jobs and extremely lucrative contracts. Famous opera singers, for example, earn $8,000 and more for each performance. Singers in an opera chorus earn between $600 and $800 per week. Classical soloists can receive between $2,000 and $3,000 per performance, while choristers may receive around $70 per performance. For rock singers, earnings can be far higher. Within the overall group of professional singers, studio and opera singers tend to earn salaries that are well respected in the industry; their opportunities for steady, long-term contracts tend to be better than for singers in other areas.

Average salaries for musicians, singers, and related workers were $37,253 in 2004, according to the U.S. Department of Labor. The lowest paid 10 percent earned less than $13,541 per year, while the highest paid 10 percent earned more than $109,990 annually.

Top studio and opera singers earn an average of $70,000 per year, though some earn much more. Rock singers may begin by playing for drinks and meals only; if successful, they may earn tens of thousands of dollars for a single performance. Singers on cruise ships generally earn between $750 and $2,000 per week, although these figures can vary considerably. Also, many singers supplement their performance earnings by working at other positions, such as teaching at schools or giving private lessons or even working at jobs unrelated to singing. The U.S. Department of Labor reports that median salaries in 2004 for full-time teachers were as follows: elementary, $43,660; middle school, $44,180; and high school, $46,120. Full-time college music teachers earned an average of $49,740 in 2004.

Because singers rarely work for a single employer, they generally receive no fringe benefits, and must provide their own health insurance and retirement planning.

Songwriters' earnings vary widely, from next to nothing to many millions of dollars. A beginning songwriter may work for free, or for low pay, just to gain experience. A songwriter may sell a jingle to an advertising agency for $1,000 or may receive many thousands of dollars if his or her work is well known. Royalties from a song may reach $20,000 per year or more per song, and a successful songwriter may earn $100,000 or more per year from the royalties of several songs. A songwriter's earnings may come from a combination of royalties earned on songs and fees earned from commercial projects.

Those starting as assistants in music production companies or jingle houses may earn as little as $20,000 per year. Experienced songwriters at these companies may earn $50,000 per year or more.

Because most songwriters are freelance, they will have to provide their own health insurance, life insurance, and pension plans. They are usually paid per project, and therefore receive no overtime pay. When facing a deadline, they may have to work many more hours than eight hours a day or 40 hours a week. Also, songwriters are generally responsible for recording their own demos and must pay for studio recording time, studio musicians, and production expenses.

WHAT IS THE JOB OUTLOOK?

Any employment forecast for singers and songwriters will most probably emphasize one factor that plays an important role in the availability of jobs: competition. Because so many people pursue musical careers and because there tend to be no formal requirements for employment in this industry (the main qualification is talent), competition is often very strong.

According to the U.S. Department of Labor, employment for singers and songwriters, as well as for musicians in general, is expected to grow about as fast as the average for all other occupations through 2014. The entertainment industry is expected to grow during the next decade, which will create jobs for singers, songwriters, and other performers. Very few people work full time in these careers. Thus, it is often advised that those who are intent on pursuing a singing or songwriting career keep in mind the varied fields other than performance in which their interest in music can be beneficial, such as education, broadcasting, therapy, and community arts management.

Related Jobs

- actors
- fiction writers
- music conductors and directors
- music producers
- musicians
- playwrights
- poets
- screenwriters

Those intent on pursuing singing careers in rock, jazz, and other popular forms should understand the keen competition they will face. There are thousands of singers all hoping to make it; only a very few actually succeed. However, there are many opportunities to perform in local cities and communities, and those with a genuine love of singing and performing should also possess a strong sense of commitment and dedication to their art.

Although songwriters face an extremely competitive job market, there are a few bright spots for those considering the field. The recent rise of independent filmmaking has created more venues for songwriters to compose film scores. Cable television also provides more opportunities for songwriting, both in the increased number of advertisements and in the growing trend for cable networks to develop their own original programs.

Many computer games and software feature songs and music, and this area should grow rapidly in the next decade. Another boom area is the World Wide Web. As more and more companies, organizations, and individuals set up multimedia Web sites, there will be an increased demand for songwriters to create songs and music for these sites. Songwriters with MIDI capability will be in the strongest position to benefit from the growth created by computer uses of music. In another field, legalized gambling has spread to many states in the country, a large number of resorts and theme parks have opened, and as these venues produce their own musical theater and shows, they will require more songwriters (and singers).

Success in songwriting is a combination of hard work, industry connections, and good luck. The number of hit songs is very small compared to the number of songwriters trying to write them.

SECTION 3

Do It Yourself

Your love of music can carry over to a successful career in many fields ranging from performance to education to health care. While talented musicians and singers have many more venues in which to perform their craft, this is still quite a competitive industry. This section will provide you with tips on how to explore the field, get additional training, and find ways to break into this growing industry. Doing so will certainly keep you an octave above the competition!

❑ TAKE HIGH SCHOOL MUSIC CLASSES

Prepare for a career in the music industry by tailoring your high school curriculum to focus on music-related classes. Besides formal music or voice instruction, there are other academic areas of study that will help you succeed. For example, if you are interested in pursuing music therapy, you will need a solid foundation in health and the sciences, especially psychology. If you want to become a music teacher, you will need an education background, as well as musical training. If you aspire to be a professional singer or musician, business classes such as accounting and marketing will prove helpful in teaching you money management skills and business acumen.

Other subjects or classes are too specialized, and may not be offered by a traditional high school. If you are truly serious about a future career in music, perhaps you may want to consider attending a performing arts high school, or take additional training outside of your school set-

ting. One such high school is The School for Creative & Performing Arts, which is located in Cincinnati, Ohio. Visit its Web site, http://scpa.cps-k12.org, for more information.

❑ PARTICIPATE IN MUSIC-RELATED ACTIVITIES

Perhaps your interest in a music career stems from the music lessons you took when you were very young. If this was something that you enjoyed, try learning how to play a new instrument, or pick up the old one.

Looking for a way to cultivate your love of music and meet new friends with similar interests? Then join a school music or performance club. Most, if not all, high schools have traditional organizations such as band, choir, and orchestra. Why not try out for the swing chorale, which combines dance performance with song, or join the jazz band, or chamber orchestra? It's a great way to learn how to play an instrument or train vocally, as well as gain experience with public performance.

Look outside of the school setting for music or performance clubs in your town or nearby city. Most park districts or community colleges have theater groups that perform plays or give recitals a few times a year.

Are you already a talented pianist (or other type of musician), with years of formal lessons under your belt? If so, you might want to give lessons to young children in your neighborhood. Beginning piano lessons focus on familiarity with the keyboard, simple songs and scales, and basic fingering. Set your teaching fee considerably lower than, say, what your own instructor would charge, dig up your old piano lesson books, and your music business is up and running. Many parents would welcome a piano teacher located so close to home, as well as the discounted lesson fee.

❏ JOIN A MUSIC ASSOCIATION

Many associations at the state and national level offer discounted memberships for interested students. With membership status you can access recent innovations or techniques used in the field, attend conferences and seminars, participate in discussion forums, and receive industry discounts or publications. Contact the association you are interested in joining to find out if it offers student membership, or search the Internet for a list of associations catering to various disciplines in the music industry.

❏ JOIN A PERFORMANCE TROUPE

Another way to learn more about music and showcase your talents is by joining a performance troupe. Many local park districts or community centers have a children's performance troupe that meets to produce and perform original musicals as well as reprisals of many Broadway favorites. Troupe members learn the basics of staging a show, from casting roles to reworking a score. Many junior high and high schools hold musicals produced and

performed by students. This is a great way to experience live performance, and hone your singing or songwriting skills.

❏ ATTEND SUMMER MUSIC CAMPS AND PROGRAMS

Use your time away from school to hone your music skills, or develop new ones. There are many summer programs and camps specially geared for musically gifted students, and focus on a variety of instruments or music disciplines. Some are highly intensive, while others focus on music, but still leave room for the usual activities associated with a summer camp, such as swimming and bonfires. Find a program that best fits your goals and age group. Ask your school music teacher and instructor if they have any recommendations on summer programs. Perhaps your school, local park district, or community college already has a program in place! If not, check the Internet for camps held near your town. Start your search by visiting http://www.kidscamps.com and http://www.astaweb.com/conferences/ SummerCamps.htm. These Web sites provide links and summaries of music and performance arts camps throughout the country.

❏ TAKE FIELD TRIPS TO MUSICAL PERFORMANCES AND MUSIC MUSEUMS

Attend live performances to learn more about different genres of music and dance. While tickets to some professional performances may be expensive, most venues offer discounts for students and teachers, as well as discounted rates for large groups. You can also opt for matinee shows for the opera and Broadway shows. Another option is to attend productions sponsored by colleges and universities, performing arts schools, or smaller theaters. Many such productions are quite elaborate and equal in caliber to those given by professional troupes. Also inquire if the theater or auditorium offers backstage tours or educational seminars. This is a great way to learn how a musical or ballet is staged, or how different sections of the orchestra come together for a performance. Contact the education or public relations department of theaters and symphonies to get more information.

It's also important to learn the history of music and instruments. What better way to learn of its evolution than by visiting music museums! There are museums located throughout the United States catering to a specific instrument or specialized field. Here are two interesting options:

- National Music Museum and Center for Study of the History of Musical Instruments. Located on the campus of the University of South Dakota, this museum holds a vast collection of antique instruments, some dating back to the 1700s. You can view its collection of pianos and learn how the simple harpsichord and pianoforte evolved to the grand pianos used by many symphonies and opera houses today. The museum also has a rich collection of tools used in making and tuning instruments. Aside from the displays, many people visit the museum to attend seminars, recording sessions, and concerts. For more information, visit http://www.usd.edu/smm/identity.html.

- Lyon & Healy Inc. If you are an aspiring harpist, you can arrange to tour the Lyon & Healy harp factory, which is located in Chicago, Illinois. A tour is given daily and shows harp students the various steps—from stringing the intricate base and frame to finishing with decorative gilding—needed to make this renowned instrument. Lyon & Healy is also a popular venue for harp concerts. Visit its Web site, http://www.lyonhealy.com, for upcoming concerts and recitals or to book a factory tour.

❏ INTERVIEW OR JOB SHADOW A PROFESSIONAL

What's the best way to learn about a career in the music industry? From professionals already established and working in the industry! Here are a few ideas to get started:

- Interview your school's orchestra or band director, or perhaps your music teacher. You can ask about their daily schedule, job responsibilities, major in college, and musical training, just to name a few questions. You can also speak with professional musicians. You can ask them how they market their musical talent. Do they use an agent? Are there peak or slow times for their particular industry? What are the pros and cons of being a musician?

- Does the field of music therapy interest you? If so, contact a local hospital, correctional facility, or other places that employ such therapists to see if you can arrange a job shadowing session. By spending even part of the workday with a music therapist, you can learn the skills and responsibilities involved with the job. Be aware that you may not be able to take part in clinical sessions due to recent changes in patient confidentiality laws. Contact the American Music Therapy Association (http://www.musictherapy.org) for a list of possible job shadowing candidates.

- The Lyric Opera of Chicago offers educational opportunities to students ranging from discounted matinee performances, backstage tours, and operas specially produced to appeal to a younger audience. They even have a "Meet the Artist" program, which allows students to meet a professional singer and learn about the education and training needed to become a professional opera singer. If you want to schedule a "Meet the Artist" session at your school, or learn more about the Lyric's educational programs, visit http://www.lyricopera.org. If you don't live in the Chicago area, similar programs in a variety of musical genres are available near you. Check with musical organizations in your area for available programs.

❑ DEMONSTRATE YOUR TALENTS IN A MUSIC COMPETITION

Music or vocal competitions are other ways to get your talents noticed, gain experience with public performance, and perhaps win some prizes to boot! Competitions can be small and local, such as a school talent show or town music contest. They can also be serious matches for national titles, scholarships, and cash prizes, with equally serious competitors. Contact the following organizations for information on their competitions or see the section, "Get Involved: A Directory of Camps, Programs, and Competitions" for details:

- American String Teachers Association (http://www.astaweb.com/competitions/BassCompetition.htm)
- MENC: The National Association for Music Education (http://www.menc.org/)
- Music Teachers National Association (http://www.mtna.org/competitions.htm)
- National Association of Composers, USA (http://www.music-usa.org/nacusa)
- Sphinx Organization (http://www.sphinxmusic.org)
- USA Songwriting Competition (http://www.songwriting.net)

❑ LAND AN INTERNSHIP

Internships in the music industry are plentiful, but available mostly to college students or recent graduates. Still, its not too early to research internships that appeal to you. After all, internships are a great way to break into the industry. How do you go about finding an internship? If you are a college student, such positions are often posted at college career centers, but are hard to obtain due to stiff competition. Rather, investigate on your own—and avoid competing with many students applying for one position. If you are in high school, the best way to find an internship is to contact employers that seem interesting to you to see what internships are available. Do you want to work for a record label? The symphony? MTV? Employers are always eager for hard workers. Also, market yourself, your talents, and your aspirations wherever you go and with whomever you come across. Industry workers and executives often frequent clubs, concerts, and performances. If you form a connection with someone from the inside, it could be your ticket to a dream internship!

Also, do your research on the Internet. Many employers post internship opportunities, including job descriptions, on their Web sites. For example, NBC Universal (http://www.nbcuni.com/About_NBC_Universal/Careers) offers internships in many of its divisions, ranging from theme parks to recording studios. Interns are responsible for a variety of tasks ranging from clerical work and assisting theme park characters, to production work at a video shoot.

❑ GET A JOB!

Part-time employment is a great way to get experience in the music industry. As a clerk in a music store, your responsibilities may include stocking and selling merchandise, such as sheet music, instruments, and accessories. You might also be asked to schedule music lessons, place special orders, and handle instrument rentals.

Part-time work at a local radio or cable station can also provide valuable work experience, as well as access to important industry contacts. You may be asked to answer phone calls, gather tracks for upcoming play lists, organize videos, or help producers with clerical tasks.

Contact local film or music studios to see if they are in need of part-time help. At first you may be doing reception work or simple clerical tasks. Hopefully, after some experience you will be able to move on to more hands-on assignments, such as helping to book music talent, editing film for videos, or picking background music for commercials.

The local paper, or your school's guidance counselor or music teacher, may be able to provide some leads for part-time work. Or you can be more aggressive and contact the human resource department of a company that seems especially appealing.

SECTION 4

What Can I Do Right Now?

Get Involved: A Directory of Camps, Programs, and Competitions

Now that you've read about some of the different careers available in music, you may be anxious to experience this line of work for yourself, to find out what it's really like. Or, perhaps you already feel certain that this is the career path for you and you're already playing an instrument or investigating nonperformance opportunities in the field. Whichever is the case, this section is for you! There are plenty of things you can do right now to learn about music careers while gaining valuable experience. Just as important, you'll get to meet new friends and see new places, too.

In the following pages you will find 34 programs run by organizations that want to work with young people interested in music. All of them can help you turn your interest into a career, but none of them will prevent you from changing your mind or just keeping your options open. Some organizations offer just one kind of program: colleges, quite naturally, will probably offer only academic courses of study. Other organizations, such as the Lyric Opera of Chicago, may offer educational programs and volunteer positions. It's up to you to decide whether you're interested in one particular type of program or are open to a number of possibilities. The kinds of activities available are listed right after the name of the program

or organization, so you can skim through to find the listings that interest you most.

❏ THE CATEGORIES

Camps

When you see an activity that is classified as a camp, don't automatically start packing your tent and mosquito repellent. Where academic study is involved, the term "camp" often simply means a residential program including both educational and recreational activities. It's sometimes hard to differentiate between such camps and other study programs, but if the sponsoring organization calls it a camp, so do we! For an extended list of camps, visit http://www.astaweb. com/conferences/SummerCamps.htm or http://www.kidscamps.com.

College Courses/Summer Study

These terms are linked because most college courses offered to students your age must take place in the summer, when you are out of school. At the same time, many colleges and universities that want to attract future students and give them a head start in higher education sponsor summer study programs. Summer study of almost any type is a good idea because it keeps your mind and your study skills sharp over the long vacation. Summer study at a college offers any number of additional benefits, including giving you the tools to make a well-informed decision about your future academic career.

Competitions

Competitions are fairly self-explanatory. They involve competition (via audio recordings you make of your work, a written composition or essay, or a live performance) with other music-minded individuals for cash prizes, opportunities to play in professional settings, or other awards. We have listed several national competitions in this book, but you will find that there are countless others available at the state and local levels. Your guidance counselor or music teacher can help you start searching in your area.

Employment and Internship Opportunities

As you may already know from experience, employment opportunities for teenagers can be very limited. Even internships are most often reserved for college students who have completed at least one or two years of study in the field. Still, if you're very determined to find an internship or paid position in music, there may be ways to find one. See Section 3: Do It Yourself in this book for some suggestions.

Field Experience

This is something of a catchall category for activities that don't exactly fit the other descriptions. But anything called a field experience in this book is always a good opportunity to get out and explore the work of music professionals.

Membership

When an organization is in this category, it simply means that you are welcome to pay your dues and become a card-carrying member. Formally joining any organization brings the benefits of meeting others who share your interests, finding opportunities to get involved, and keeping up with current events. Depending on how active you are, the contacts you make and the experiences you gain may help when the time comes to apply to colleges or look for a job.

In some organizations, you pay a special student rate and receive benefits similar to regular members. Many organizations, however, are now starting student branches with their own benefits and publications. As in any field, make sure you understand exactly what the benefits of membership are before you join.

Finally, don't let membership dues discourage you from making contact with these organizations. Some charge dues as low as $10 because they know that students are perpetually short of funds. When the annual dues are higher, think of the money as an investment in your future and then consider if it is too much to pay.

❑ PROGRAM DESCRIPTIONS

Once you've started to look at the individual listings themselves, you'll find that they contain a lot of information. Naturally, there is a general description of each program, but wherever possible we also have included the following details.

Application Information

Each listing notes how far in advance you'll need to apply for the program or position, but the simple rule is to apply as far in advance as possible. This ensures that you won't miss out on a great opportunity simply because other people got there ahead of you. It also means that you will get a timely decision on your application, so if you are not accepted, you'll still have some time to apply elsewhere. As for the things that make up your application—audition tapes, essays, recommendations, etc.—we've tried to cover what's involved, but be sure to contact the program about specific requirements before you submit anything.

Background Information

This includes such information as the name of the organization that is sponsoring it financially and the faculty and staff who will be there for you. This can help you—and your family—gauge the quality and reliability of the program.

Classes and Activities

Classes and activities change from year to year, depending on popularity, availability of instructors, and many other factors. Nevertheless, colleges and universities quite consistently offer the same or similar classes, even in their summer sessions. Courses like "Music Theory" and "Introduction to Music History," for example, are simply indispensable. So you can look through the listings and see which programs offer foundational courses like these and which offer courses on more variable topics. As for

activities, we note when you have access to recreational facilities on campus, and it's usually a given that special social and cultural activities will be arranged for most programs.

Contact Information

Wherever possible, we have given the title of the person whom you should contact instead of the name because people change jobs so frequently. If no title is given and you are telephoning an organization, simply tell the person who answers the phone the name of the program that interests you and he or she will forward your call. If you are writing, include the line "Attention: Summer Study Program" (or whatever is appropriate after "Attention") somewhere on the envelope. This will help to ensure that your letter goes to the person in charge of that program.

Credit

Where academic programs are concerned, we sometimes note that high school or college credit is available to those who have completed them. This means that the program can count toward your high school diploma or a future college degree just like a regular course. Obviously, this can be very useful, but it's important to note that rules about accepting such credit vary from school to school. Before you commit to a program offering high school credit, check with your guidance counselor to see if it is acceptable to your school. As for programs offering college credit, check with your chosen college (if you have one) to see if they will accept it.

Eligibility and Qualifications

The main eligibility requirement to be concerned about is age or grade in school. A term frequently used in relation to grade level is "rising," as in "rising senior": someone who will be a senior when the next school year begins. This is especially important where summer programs are concerned. A number of university-based programs make admissions decisions partly in consideration of GPA, class rank, and standardized test scores. This is mentioned in the listings, but you must contact the program for specific numbers. If you are worried that your GPA or your ACT scores, for example, aren't good enough, don't let them stop you from applying to programs that consider such things in the admissions process. Often, a fine essay, a top-quality audition tape, or even an example of your dedication and eagerness can compensate for statistical weaknesses.

Facilities

We tell you where you'll be living, studying, eating, and having fun during these programs, but there isn't enough room to go into all the details. Some of those details can be important: what is and isn't accessible for people with disabilities, whether the site of a summer program has air-conditioning, and how modern the performance facilities are. You can expect most program brochures and application materials to address these concerns, but if you still have questions about the facilities, just call the program's administration and ask.

Financial Details

While a few of the programs listed here are fully underwritten by collegiate and corporate sponsors, most of them rely on you for at least some of their funding. The 2006 prices and fees are given here, but you should bear in mind that costs rise slightly almost every year. You and your parents must take costs into consideration when choosing a program. We always try to note where financial aid is available, but really, most programs will do their best to ensure that a shortage of funds does not prevent you from taking part.

Residential vs. Commuter Options

Simply put, some programs prefer that participating students live with other participants and staff members, others do not, and still others leave the decision entirely to the students themselves. As a rule, residential programs are suitable for young people who live out of town or even out of state, as well as for local residents. They generally provide a better overview of college life than programs in which you're only on campus for a few hours a day, and they're a way to test how well you cope with living away from home. Commuter programs may be viable only if you live near the program site or if you can stay with relatives who do. Bear in mind that for residential programs especially, the travel between your home and the location of the activity is almost always your responsibility and can significantly increase the cost of participation.

❏ FINALLY . . .

Ultimately, there are three important things to bear in mind concerning all of the programs listed in this volume. The first is that things change. Staff members come and go, funding is added or withdrawn, supply and demand determine which programs continue and which terminate. Dates, times, and costs vary widely due to a number of factors. Because of this, the information we give you, although as current and detailed as possible, is just not enough on which to base your final decision. If you are interested in a program, you simply must write, call, fax, or e-mail the organization concerned to get the latest and most complete information available. This has the added benefit of putting you in touch with someone who can deal with your individual questions and problems.

Another important point to keep in mind when considering these programs is that the people who run them provided the information printed here. The editors of this book haven't attended the programs and don't endorse them: we simply give you the information with which to begin your own research. And after all, we can't pass judgment because you're the only one who can decide which programs are right for you.

The final thing to bear in mind is that the programs listed here are just the tip of the iceberg. No book can possibly cover all of the opportunities that are available to you—partly because they are so numerous and are constantly coming and going, and partly because some are waiting to be discovered. For instance, you may be very interested in taking a college course but don't see the college that interests you in the listings. Call their admissions office! Even if they don't have a special program for high school students, they might be able to make some kind of arrangements for you to visit or sit in on a class. Use the ideas behind these listings and take the initiative to turn them into opportunities!

❏ THE PROGRAMS

Academic Study Associates (ASA)
College Courses/Summer Study

Academic Study Associates has been offering residential and commuter pre-college summer programs for young people for more than 20 years. It offers college credit classes and enrichment opportunities in a variety of academic fields, including performing arts, at the University of Massachusetts–Amherst, as well as institutions abroad. In addition to classroom work, students participate in field trips, mini-clinics, and extracurricular activities. Programs are usually three to four weeks in length. Fees and deadlines vary for these programs—visit the ASA's Web site for further details. Options are also available for middle school students.

Academic Study Associates (ASA)
ASA Programs
375 West Broadway, Suite 200
New York, NY 10012-4324
800-752-2250
summer@asaprograms.com
http://www.asaprograms.com/home/
    asa_home.asp

American Institute for Foreign Study's Summer Advantage Program

College Courses/Summer Study

The American Institute for Foreign Study offers the Summer Advantage Program study abroad program for high school students who are interested in foreign language, culture, and other subjects. Applicants must be at least 16 years of age, have completed their sophomore year, and have a GPA of at least 2.5. Educational programs are available in China, England, France, Italy, Russia, and Spain. Students are immersed in the artistic and cultural history of their host countries, while taking up to eight credit hours. Students interested in music might want to pursue study in London, England, where they can take "Introduction to Modern Popular Music." In addition to credit courses, enrichment courses are also offered at all locations. Contact the institute for more information on program fees. Scholarships are available.

American Institute for Foreign Study
Summer Programs
River Plaza
9 West Broad Street
Stamford, CT 06902-3788
800-913-7151
summeradvantage@aifs.com
http://www.summeradvantage.com

American String Teachers Association (ASTA)

Competitions

The ASTA offers two competitions to young people who play stringed instruments: the Auday-Giormenti Double Bass Competition and the National Solo Competition. Applicants for the Auday-Giormenti Double Bass Competition must be between the ages of 12 and 21, and either the applicant or his or her teacher must be a member of the ASTA. Applicants must submit a completed application packet, plus three copies (of all materials). The application packet consists of a completed application along with an audio CD and a videotape of a specific concerto/concertos. Visit the association's Web site for a list of approved selections. Applicants must also submit a second piece of their own choice, which should be contrasting in style to the required selection. A $25 entry fee is also required. Winners receive an Auday-Giormenti Viennese model double bass, a brief performance at the ASTA National Conference, and a commemorative plaque.

Two competition divisions are available for those interested in the National Solo Competition. Applicants for the junior division must be under the age of 19, and applicants for the senior division must be ages 19 to 25. Applicants must be soloists on one of the following instruments: violin, viola, cello, double bass, classical guitar, or harp. They must also be ASTA members or current students of ASTA members. Applicants must first register for their state competition. Finalists from the state competition advance to the national competition. Applicants should contact their ASTA State Competition Chairs for information about entering their state competition. A complete list of these state chairs is available on the

ASTA's Web site. Detailed information about repertoire choices for the national event is listed on the Web site. Visit the Web site to read more about the competition and to locate your state contact.

American String Teachers Association (ASTA)
4153 Chain Bridge Road
Fairfax, VA 22030
703-279-2113
http://www.astaweb.com/ competitions/BassCompetition. htm and http://www.astaweb. com/2007/SoloComp.html

The Arts! At Maryland at the University of Maryland
College Course/Summer Study
Motivated high school juniors and seniors may participate in The Arts! At Maryland, a three-week exploration of the creative arts at the University of Maryland. Each July, participants can interact with teachers and other professionals and take one three-credit course in creative writing, dance, music, theater arts, or visual arts. Recent music courses included "Introduction to Music Technology" and "The Jazz Experience." Students are encouraged to share their talents at student cabaret coffee houses, which are held at the Kogod Theatre at the Clarice Smith Performing Arts Center. Participants live in the residence halls at the University of Maryland and take their meals on campus or in selected College Park restaurants. A commuter option is also available. To apply, you must submit an application form, an essay, two letters of recommendation, a current transcript, and an application fee of $55 by mid-May. Cost for the residential option is approximately $2,719; cost for the commuter option is $1,719. For further details and an application form, visit the Web site listed below or contact the Summer Sessions and Special Programs staff.

University of Maryland
Summer Sessions and Special Programs
Mitchell Building, 1st Floor
College Park, MD 20742-0001
301-314-8240
http://www.summer.umd.edu/s/taam

Buck's Rock Performing and Creative Arts Camp
Camps
Buck's Rock Camp, about 85 miles from New York, has been in existence since 1942. It features more than 30 different activities in creative, performing, and visual arts. The camp has its very own state-of-the-art recording studio. Here, you can work with audio engineers to produce your own CDs. In addition to the recording studio, there are many other opportunities for those interested in music of any style. Ensembles are available in orchestra, choir, jazz band, chamber music, jazz vocals, and men's and women's a cappella singing groups. One of the camp's most popular events is Rock Café, where up to 35 camper bands perform under an open-air tent for counselors and fellow campers.

Buck's Rock Camp is for 11- to 16-year-olds who are artistic, talented, and independent. At camp, you make your own schedule and participate in as many activities as you want to. Many students return to Buck's Rock year after year and go on to become counselors. If you're 16 to 18 years old, you can register for the Counselors-in-Training program and spend part of your day as a camper and part as a counselor. In this program, you receive a reduction in camp tuition.

Buck's Rock Camp has two four-week sessions and one eight-week session. Tuition for four weeks costs $5,790; the full season costs $7,960. This includes everything but transportation to the camp. Campers stay in cabins, eat in the dining room, and enjoy a full schedule of evening activities. You can get financial aid to help with tuition, and Buck's Rock likes to help as many campers as possible. To apply to the camp, you must fill out an enrollment form and attend a personal interview. To get your form, and to learn more, call, write, or e-mail the camp. You can also visit its Web site.

Buck's Rock Camp
59 Buck Rock Road
New Milford, CT 06776-5311
800-636-5218
bucksrock@bucksrockcamp.com
http://www.bucksrockcamp.com

Camp Ballibay
Camps

Camp Ballibay, established in 1964, is accredited by the American Camping Association. It offers programs (two to nine weeks in length) in music, rock and roll, jazz, video, radio, art, photography, theater, and horseback riding for students ages six to 16. Campers in the music program, for example, learn about the field via traditional vocal, string, woodwind, and brass training; workshops and classes; and ensemble opportunities including duets, trios, and quartets, improvisational groups, and vocal jazz ensembles. Campers stay in cabins and have access to a swimming pool, a riding area, tennis courts, sports fields, an infirmary, a camp store, and a dining hall. Tuition for this residential camp ranges from $1,950 to $6,250, depending on the length of the program. Contact Camp Ballibay for further information.

Camp Ballibay
One Ballibay Road
Camptown, PA 18815
570-746-3223
jannone@ballibay.com
http://www.ballibay.com

Early Experience Program at the University of Denver
College Course/Summer Study

The University of Denver invites academically gifted high school students interested in music and other subjects to apply for its Early Experience Program, which involves participating in university-level classes during the school year and especially during the summer. This is a commuter-only program. Interested students must submit a completed application (with essay), official high school transcript, standardized test results (PACT/ACT/PSAT/SAT), a letter of recommendation from a counselor or teacher, and have a minimum GPA of 3.0. Contact the Early Experience program coordinator for more information, including application forms, available classes, and current fees.

University of Denver
Office of Academic Youth Programs
Early Experience Program
Attn: Pam Campbell, Coordinator
1981 South University Boulevard
Denver, CO 80208-4209
303-871-2663
pcampbe1@du.edu
http://www.du.edu/education/ces/
    ee.html

Exploration Summer Programs (ESP) at Yale University
College Course/Summer Study
Exploration Summer Programs has been offering academic summer enrichment programs to students for nearly 30 years. Rising high school sophomores, juniors, and seniors can participate in ESP's Senior Program at Yale University. Two three-week residential and day sessions are available and are typically held in June and July. Participants can choose from more than 80 courses in the performing arts and other areas of study. Recent classes included "West African Rhythms: Drumming + Percussion," "Bare Bones of Music: Music Theory + Composition," "No Business Like Show Business: Musical Theatre," "STOMP!: Percussion + Movement," "School of Rock: Musical Development," and "No Instruments Allowed: A Cappella." Students also take college seminars, which provide course work that is similar to that of first-year college study. All courses and seminars are ungraded and not-for-credit. In addition to academics, students participate in extracurricular activities such as tours, sports, concerts, weekend recreational trips, college trips, and discussions of current events and other issues. Tuition for the Residential Senior Program is approximately $4,345 for one session and $8,000 for two sessions. A limited number of need-based partial and full scholarships are available. Programs are also available for students in grades four through nine. Contact ESP for more information.

Exploration Summer Programs
470 Washington Street, PO Box 368
Norwood, MA 02062-0368
781-762-7400
http://www.explo.org

Friday Morning Music Club
Competitions, Membership
Young women and men singers, composers, pianists, and string players who are preparing for a professional career are eligible to compete in the Washington International Competition for Singers. Competitions are announced through secondary and postsecondary institutions, music teachers, and music publications. Applicants must submit an audition CD. Those who are accepted compete in Washington, DC, before a panel of judges who determine category winners. Awards range from $2,000 to $7,000.

Students between the ages of 14 and 22 may also apply for membership in the club via musical auditions. Audition categories include Solo Piano and Other Instruments, Piano Accompaniment, Chamber Ensemble, Composition, and Voice. Contact the club for more information.

Friday Morning Music Club

2233 Wisconsin Avenue, NW,
Suite 326
Washington, DC 20007-4126
202-333-2075
fmmc@fmmc.org
http://www.fmmc.org/students/index.html

Hershey's All-USA High School Musicians Competition

Competition

Sophomore, junior, and senior high school musicians are eligible to be nominated as one of the top 100 high school-age musicians in the United States. Hershey Foods and MENC: The National Association for Music Education created the competition jointly. Applicants must be enrolled in their school's music program, demonstrate exceptional musical talent, maintain a GPA of at least 3.0, and be in good academic standing. Their music directors and teachers nominate students. Those who advance to the semifinalist level must submit recorded auditions to the Washington, DC-based Army Bands, which select the finalists. Winners do not play together as a group, but receive national recognition for their abilities. Some winners are eligible for scholarships. There is an application fee of $20. Contact MENC for more information.

Hershey's All-USA High School Musicians

c/o MENC: The National
Association for Music Education
All-USA High School Musicians
1806 Robert Fulton Drive
Reston, VA 20191-5462
800-336-3768
gretchenr@menc.org
http://www.menc.org/contest/allusa/2006/06faq.html

High School Honors Program at Boston University

College Course/Summer Study

Two summer educational opportunities are available for high school students interested in music and other majors. Rising high school seniors can participate in the High School Honors Program, which offers six-week, for-credit undergraduate study at the university. Students take two for-credit classes (up to eight credits) alongside regular Boston College students, live in dorms on campus, and participate in extracurricular activities and tours of local attractions. Recent classes included "Elements of Music Theory," "Piano," "Violin," "Viola," and "Voice." The program typically begins in early July. Students who demonstrate financial need may be eligible for financial aid. Tuition for the program is approximately $3,750, with registration/program fees ($350) and room and board options ($1,701 to $1,832) extra. Note: Additional fees may be required for music classes.

Boston University Summer Programs

755 Commonwealth Avenue
Boston, MA 02215-1401

617-353-5124
summer@bu.edu
http://www.bu.edu/summer/high_
    school/index.html

Interlochen Arts Camp
Camp

Interlochen, located near scenic Traverse City, Michigan, is one of the premier art camps in the United States for young musicians, visual artists, dancers, actors, and writers. Young people in grades 3 through 12 who are interested in music can participate in summer music programs. Students in the High School Division (grades 9 through 12) may "major" in one of the following areas: orchestra, string quartet, winds, jazz, piano, organ, harp, composition, guitar, or voice. Programs last one, four, or six weeks. The tuition for this camp varies by program length ($750 for one week; $4,088 for four weeks; and $5,802, $5,892, and $6,002 for six weeks depending on the major), but includes classes, room and board, group instruction, required private lessons, use of all recreational facilities, and admission to student and faculty performances.

Interlochen also offers a two-week All-State Summer Music Camp to musically gifted Michigan residents who have completed grade 8, 9, 10, 11, or 12 before the summer of the program. Programs are available in band, orchestra, or choir. Campers get the opportunity to learn from music professionals and interact with other musically gifted students. Cost of the program is $1,200, which includes classes, room and board, group instruc-tion, required private lessons, use of all recreational facilities, and admission to student and faculty performances.

Students in both programs stay in cabins with 10 to 18 other campers and counselors and have access to a private beach, tennis courts, division headquarters, and laundry (students are required to do their own laundry). Extracurricular activities include concerts by well-known musicians, dances, viewing gallery exhibits, arts and crafts, sports, and outdoor activities. The camp has eight major performance sites, dozens of performing ensembles, and more than 25 performances by distinguished guest artists. Financial aid is available based on the financial need and the musical talent of the applicant. Applications for these programs are due in February. Contact the camp for more information.

Interlochen Arts Camp
Admissions Office
PO Box 199
Interlochen, MI 49643-0199
800-681-5912
admissions@interlochen.org
http://www.interlochen.org/camp/
    summer_camp_programs

Intern Exchange International Ltd.
Employment and Internship Opportunities

High school students ages 16 to 18 (including graduating seniors) can participate in a month-long Career-Plus-Programmes in London, England. Options are available in theater, video production, and other areas. Students learn about these fields via hands-on experience and workshop instruction. The cost of the program is approximately $6,245, plus airfare; this fee includes tuition, housing (students live in residence halls at the University of London), breakfast and dinner daily, housekeeping service, linens and towels, special dinner events, weekend trips and excursions, group activities including scheduled theatre, and a Tube Pass. Contact Intern Exchange International for more information.

Intern Exchange International Ltd.
2606 Bridgewood Circle
Boca Raton, FL 33434-4118
561-477-2434
info@internexchange.com
http://www.internexchange.com

Long Lake Camp for the Arts
Camps
Long Lake Camp for the Arts offers a variety of arts-based programs to young people ages 10 through 16. Programs include Music, Fine Arts, Theatre, Dance, Circus, and Video/Film. The Music program offers a variety of experiential opportunities to campers, whether they are interested in playing in a band, performing in an orchestra, singing in a chorus, or learning how to play an instrument. To demonstrate their skills and have a little fun, campers play for the rest of the camp each Friday, Saturday, and Sunday. In addition to program-related activities, campers can participate in sports and outdoor recreational outings. Three- and six-week sessions are available and cost

$4,450 and $7,950, respectively. Tuition includes food and lodging, private lessons, craft materials, and all programs of instruction except horseback riding. Contact the camp for more information.

Long Lake Camp for the Arts
199 Washington Avenue
Dobbs Ferry, NY 10522-1212
914-693 7111
marc@longlakecamp.com
http://www.longlakecamp.com

The Lyric Opera of Chicago
Field Experience
The Lyric Opera of Chicago offers educational opportunities to students, including discounted matinee performances, backstage tours, and operas specially produced to appeal to a younger audience. They even have a Meet the Artist program, which allows students to meet a professional singer and learn about the education and training needed to become a professional opera singer. In addition, you can apply for membership in the Lyric Opera Lecture Corps. Once you receive training, you will get the opportunity to work in one of the following positions: opera lecturer at various sites in the community, Student Backstage Tour guide, high school lecturer for the organization's Student Matinee programs, lecturer for elementary school students in the organization's Opera-in-the-Classroom program, or administrative worker. Prospective Lecture Corps members do not need to have prior musical training or musical acumen, but they do need to be season subscription holders. Contact the

Lyric Opera of Chicago for more information on these programs.

Lyric Opera of Chicago
Education Department
20 North Wacker Drive
Chicago, IL 60606-2806
312-827-5912
http://www.lyricopera.org

The Museum of Television and Radio
Employment and Internship Opportunities, Membership

If you're interested in the history of television and radio, this could be the opportunity for you. The Museum of Television and Radio, with locations in New York City and Los Angeles, offers internships to high school students. The museums are happy to accept highly motivated students who possess a keen interest in the radio and television industry. You must have an eye for detail, some computer training, and the ability to work well with others. Interns often develop their own project or help the museum in a particular area in need of research. Internships are designed to meet the needs of individuals and their schools. How many hours you'll put in each week, and whether or not you'll receive high school credit, is something to work out with your career counselor. Most students work at the museum about eight hours a week for one semester. Full-year internships are also possible. School-to-work and work-study students are welcome. Interns commute to the museums, and no residential facilities are available.

To intern at the Los Angeles museum, call the museum directly to discuss your interests and schedule. If you live in New York City, you must submit a completed application (available at the museum's Web site), a resume, and two letters of recommendation (either academic or professional). Visit the museum's Web site for a description of intern opportunities by department. Recent listings included internship options in the curatorial, library services, public relations, publications, and research services departments.

In addition, membership opportunities are also available at the museums.

The Museum of Television and Radio
Los Angeles Branch:
Internship Program
465 North Beverly Drive
Beverly Hills, CA 90210-4601
310-786-1025
http://www.mtr.org

New York City Branch:
Internship Program
25 West 52nd Street
New York, NY 10019-6104
212-621-6615
http://www.mtr.org

Music Camps at the University of Wisconsin-Green Bay
Camps

Students interested in music may participate in the following camps offered by the University of Wisconsin-Green Bay: Vocal Jazz, Blues and Gospel Camp (for students entering grades 8 through 12); Jazz Ensemble Camp (grades

8 through 12); Middle School Band, Orchestra, and Choral Camp (grades 6 through 9); Senior High Band, Orchestra, and Choral Camp (grades 9 through 12); and Guitar Camp (grades 8 through 12). Program lengths, eligibility requirements, and application deadlines vary by camp. Contact the Office of Outreach and Extension for further information on these programs.

University of Wisconsin–Green Bay

Youth Opportunities Summer Camps
Office of Outreach and Extension
2420 Nicolet Drive
Green Bay, WI 54311-7001
800-892-2118
summercamps@uwgb.edu
http://www.uwgb.edu/camps

Music Teachers National Association Student Competition

Competition

The Music Teachers National Association (MTNA) offers five national competitions annually for elementary-age through college-level students. Competitions are available in piano, strings, brass, woodwind, and voice. Prizes vary depending on the sponsors—among them Baldwin Piano Company, Yamaha Corp. of America, and Warner Bros. Publications Inc.—but the ultimate prize is the opportunity to perform at the annual MTNA conference. Entry fees for these competitions range from $70 to $100. For competition dates and entrance qualifications, contact the association.

Music Teachers National Association

Student Competitions
441 Vine Street, Suite 505
Cincinnati, OH 45202-2811
513-421-1420
mtnanet@mtna.org
http://www.mtna.org/competitions.htm

National Association of Composers, USA (NACUSA)

Competition

Association members who are U.S. citizens or residents between the ages of 18 and 30 may participate in the Composer's Competition. Compositions must be no longer than 15 minutes in length and require no more than five players to perform. Applicants may submit up to two compositions for judging. First-prize winners receive $400, and second-prize winners, $100. Prize-winning compositions may also be performed at a NACUSA concert. Contact the NACUSA for more information.

National Association of Composers, USA

PO Box 49256, Barrington Station
Los Angeles, CA 90049-0256
310-541-8213
nacusa@music-usa.org
http://www.music-usa.org/nacusa

National High School Music Institute at Northwestern University

College Course/Summer Study

The National High School Institute is the nation's oldest university-based program for outstanding high school students. It was established in 1931. The month-long program has the following divisions: Music, Theatre Arts, Film and Video Production, Journalism, Coon-Hardy Debate Scholars, and Forensics-Individual Events. (Note: Two adjunct divisions—Junior Statesmen and Championship Debate—are also available.) Students in the Music program perform in nearly 20 concerts, take musical field trips, and participate in master classes and seminars related to performance, health in the performing arts, audition preparation, and applying to top music schools. Students in the Film & Video Production program can choose from one of two concentrations: Production or Screenwriting. Production students take core classes in camera technology, digital editing, digital design and animation, and screenwriting. Each student completes a final short project—a narrative video, documentary video, animated short, or an experimental video. The student-to-teacher ratio for these programs is six-to-one. Applicants for the Music section must be currently in 8th through 11th grades; those interested in attending the Film & Video Production section must be in 11th grade. All applicants must have at least a B average (although exceptions are made). A variety of extracurricular activities are also available to students in the program, including tours, movies, shopping, sing-alongs, and outings to sporting and cultural events. Students live on campus in university residence halls, where they also take their meals. The cost of the program is approximately $3,650, which includes tuition, room, board, health service, field

trips, and group events. Scholarships are available. Visit the program's Web site for more information.

Northwestern University
National High School Music
    Institute
617 Noyes Street
800-662-NHSI
Evanston, IL 60208-4165
nhsi@northwestern.edu
http://www.northwestern.edu/nhsi

Orchestra Fellowship Program at Michigan Technological University
College Course/Summer Study
Michigan Technological University offers the Orchestra Fellowship Program for high school students. Students take part in daily rehearsals and master classes to hone their talents. Students also get the chance to participate in the Pine Mountain Music Festival, a music festival in Michigan's Upper Peninsula. During the festival, students take part in rehearsals and performances of an opera. All students who are selected receive a scholarship, which covers all program costs, including tuition, notebooks, and room and board in a university residence hall. Participants are required to pay only for registration ($10), personal items, and transportation to and from the school.

Michigan Technological
    University
Orchestra Fellowship Program
Youth Programs Office, Alumni
    House
1400 Townsend Drive

Houghton, MI 49931-1295
906-487-2219
http://youthprograms.mtu.edu

Pre-College Division at The Julliard School

Field Experience

Highly qualified students can enrich their classical and concert musical training by attending the Pre-College Division at Julliard. The program is available to students age 7 through senior year in high school. (Note: Voice students must be at least 14.) Students enrolled in this program attend special classes on Saturdays for 30 weeks between September and May. Students benefit from class instruction on music theory and composition, and solfege (ear-training). Private music and voice lessons are taught by professors from the Julliard School. There are numerous opportunities for solo and group recitals throughout the school year. Admission to the school is selective and audition-based; students must be highly advanced musicians or vocalists to be eligible. Tuition for the program is $6,850 [plus $750 for a weekly, half-hour private lesson (per semester) or $1,500 for a weekly, one-hour private lesson (per semester)]. Students enrolled in the conducting class must pay an additional $500. For more information on the program and available scholarships, contact The Julliard School.

The Julliard School
Pre-College Division
60 Lincoln Center Plaza
New York, NY 10023-6588
212-799-5000, ext. 241

http://www.juilliard.edu/precollege/
general.html

Pre-College Program at Johns Hopkins University

College Courses/Summer Study

Johns Hopkins University welcomes academically talented high school students to its summertime Pre-College Program. Participants live on Hopkins' Homewood campus for five weeks beginning in early July. They take two courses leading to college credit; those interested in careers in the music industry should strongly consider enrolling in courses such as "Introduction to Western Classical Music," "Introduction to Business," "Business Law," "Principles of Marketing," "Business Communication," as well as in several foreign languages. All participants in the Pre-College Program also attend workshops on college admissions, time management, and diversity. Students who live in the greater Baltimore area have the option of commuting. As of July 1, applicants must be at least 15; have completed their sophomore, junior, or senior year; and have a minimum GPA of 3.0. All applicants must submit an application form, essay, transcript, two recommendations, and a non-refundable application fee (rates vary by date of submission). Contact the Office of Summer Programs for financial aid information, costs, and deadlines.

Pre-College Program
Johns Hopkins University
Office of Summer Programs
Wyman Park Building, Suite G4

3400 North Charles Street
Baltimore, MD 21218-2685
800-548-0548
summer@jhu.edu
http://www.jhu.edu/~sumprog/index.
 html

SkillsUSA
Competitions
SkillsUSA offers "local, state and national competitions in which students demonstrate occupational and leadership skills." Students who participate in its SkillsUSA Championships, and who are interested in careers in the music industry, can compete in categories such as Advertising Design, Electronics Applications, Electronics Technology, Job Interview, and Television (Video) Production. SkillsUSA works directly with high schools and colleges, so ask your guidance counselor or teacher if it is an option for you. Visit the SkillsUSA Web site for more information.

SkillsUSA
PO Box 3000
Leesburg, VA 20177-0300
703-777-8810
http://www.skillsusa.org

Society of Broadcast Engineers
Membership
The society offers youth membership ($10) to high school students who are either active in the technical operation of a broadcast station, involved in a school club or community organization such as an amateur radio club, or who have a general interest in broadcast engineer-

ing. Youth members receive the *Youth Member Newsletter,* the opportunity to interact with a mentor, and information on careers, education, scholarships, and internships. Contact the society for more information.

Society of Broadcast Engineers
9102 North Meridian Street,
 Suite 150
Indianapolis, IN 46260-1895
317-846-9000
mclappe@sbe.org
http://www.sbe.org

Songwriters Guild of America
Membership
The guild represents the professional interests of songwriters. It offers a membership option to beginning songwriters. Visit its Web site for more information.

Songwriters Guild of America
1500 Harbor Boulevard
Weehawken, NJ 07086-6732
201-867-7603
songwritersnj@aol.com
http://www.songwritersguild.com

Sphinx Organization
Competition
This organization, which promotes diversity in classical education, offers an annual competition for young African American and Hispanic American string players. Instrumental categories include violin, viola, cello, and double bass. Students in the Junior Division must not have reached their 18th birthday by a date

specified by the organization. Participants in the Senior Division must be at least 18 years of age, but not yet 27, by a date specified by the organization. Cash prizes and the opportunity to perform with the organization's orchestra, as well as with professional orchestras, are provided to winners. Semi-finalists also receive a full scholarship to attend summer music programs. For more information, contact the Screening Committee.

Sphinx Organization
Screening Committee
400 Renaissance Center, Suite 2550
Detroit, MI 48243-1679
313-877-9100
info@sphinxmusic.org
http://www.sphinxmusic.org

Summer College for High School Students at Syracuse University
College Course/Summer Study

Students who have completed their sophomore, junior, or senior year of high school are eligible to apply to the Summer College for High School Students at Syracuse University, which runs for six weeks from early July to mid-August. The program has several aims: to introduce you to the many possible majors and study areas within your interest area; to help you match your aptitudes with possible careers; and to prepare you for college, both academically and socially. Students attend classes, listen to lectures, and take field trips to destinations that are related to their specific area of interest. All students are required to take two courses during the program and they receive col-

lege credit if they successfully complete the courses.

Readers of this book should look into the Acting & Musical Theatre and Public Communications program options. In the Acting & Musical Theatre program, students develop their performance skills and learn more about music, drama, and dance as it relates to the theater. They also take the following three-credit courses, "Elements of Performance" and "Basic Acting." Students taking the Public Communications option explore the field by studying journalism, television and cable, radio, the music industry, public relations, advertising, and film. They also take two courses for credit.

Admission is competitive and is based on recommendations, test scores, and transcripts. Costs vary by program. Some scholarships are available. The application deadline is in mid-May, or mid-April for those seeking financial aid. For further information, contact the Summer College.

Syracuse University
Summer College for High School
    Students
111 Waverly Avenue, Suite 240
Syracuse, NY 13244-2320
315-443-5297
summcoll@syr.edu
http://summercollege.syr.edu

Summer Program for Secondary School Program at Harvard University
College Course/Summer Study

High school students who have completed their sophomore, junior, or senior years may apply to Harvard's Summer Program for Secondary School Program. Students who live on campus take either two four-unit courses or one eight-unit course for college credit. Commuting students may take only one four-unit course for college credit. Recent music-related courses included "The Evolution of Modern Jazz through Jazz-Rock and Fusion," "Introduction to Western Music of the Golden Era: from the Baroque to Romanticism," "Study Abroad in Venice: Microcosm of the World of Italian Music," and "Music Theory." In addition to academics, students can participate in extracurricular activities such as intramural sports, a trivia bowl, a talent show, and dances. Tuition for the program ranges from $2,200 (per four-unit course) to $4,440 (per eight-unit course). A nonrefundable registration fee ($50), health insurance ($110), and room and board (short session, $1,965; long session, $3,875) are extra. The application deadline for this program is mid-June. Contact the program for more information.

Harvard University
Summer Program for Secondary
  School Program
51 Brattle Street
Cambridge, MA 02138-3701
617-495-3192
ssp@hudce.harvard.edu
http://www.ssp.harvard.edu

Summer Study at Pennsylvania State University
College Course/Summer Study

High school students who are interested in music or other fields can apply to par-

ticipate in Penn State's three-and-a-half-week Non-Credit Enrichment Program, which is held in early July and features music-related classes such as "From Aerosmith to Zeppelin: The History Of Rock 'N Roll." Students who have completed the 9th, 10th, and 11th grades are eligible for the program. Tuition for the Non-Credit Enrichment Program is approximately $4,000. Limited financial aid is available. Contact the Summer Study Program for more information.

Penn State University
Summer Study Program
900 Walt Whitman Road
Melville, NY 11747-2293
800-666-2556
info@summerstudy.com
http://www.summerstudy.com/
  pennstate

Tri-M Music Honor Society
Membership

This organization is the only international honor society for middle and high school music students. Members are recognized for their musical talents, academic achievement, and involvement in extracurricular and community activities. The society is sponsored by MENC: The National Association for Music Education, and has 4,400 chapters worldwide. Ask your music instructor if a chapter exists at your school; if not, ask him or her to contact the society about organizing one.

Tri-M Music Honor Society
800-336-3768
http://www.menc.org/information/
  trim/main_trim.html

The USA Songwriting Competition

Competition

This competition offers one of the largest prize purses in the nation—$50,000 in cash and merchandise to its first place winner. Competition categories include Children, Country, Dance/Electronica, Folk, Gospel/Inspirational, Hip-Hop/Rap, Instrumental, Jazz, Latin, Lyrics Only, Novelty/Comedy, Pop, Rock/Alternative, R&B, and World. Songwriters submit their original work to be judged by a panel of music industry experts and executives. Along with the prize money and radio play, winners receive merchandise and services from many of the contest's sponsors such as Sony and Ibanez Guitars. An entry fee of $30 is required. For more information on this competition, visit the organization's Web site.

The USA Songwriting Competition
4331 North Federal Highway, Suite 403A
Ft. Lauderdale, FL 33308-5254
954-776-1577
info@songwriting.net
http://www.songwriting.net

Women Band Directors National Association

Membership

This organization, which represents the professional interests of female band directors, offers membership options for high school and college students. Contact the association for information on membership benefits.

Women Band Directors National Association
296 Dailey Hills Circle
Ringgold, GA 30736-8156
http://www.womenbanddirectors.org

Women In Music—National Network

Membership

This organization "promotes the development, advancement and recognition of women in the music industry." It offers two membership options for young women who are interested in music. Those who sign up for basic membership (free) receive a free newsletter, and those who sign up for silver membership ($9.95 a month) receive access to job listings, a mentor program, a resume/profile listing, songwriter resources, a newsletter, and meeting invitations. Contact the network for more information.

Women In Music—National Network
PO Box 1925
El Cerrito, CA 94530-4925
866-305-7963
admin@womeninmusic.com
http://www.womeninmusic.com

Read a Book

When it comes to finding out about music, don't overlook a book. (You're reading one now, after all.) What follows is a short, annotated list of books and periodicals related to music. The books range from insider looks at the music industry and careers in the profession, to professional volumes on specific topics, such as audio recording technology. Don't be afraid to check out the professional journals, either. Those that are technically oriented may be way above your head right now, but if you take the time to become familiar with one or two, you're bound to pick up some of what is important to music professionals, not to mention begin to feel like you're a part of their world, which is what you're interested in, right?

We've tried to include recent materials as well as old favorites. Always check for the most recent editions, and, if you find an author you like, ask your librarian to help you find more. Keep reading good books!

❏ BOOKS

Austin, Dave, Mary Ellen Bickford, and Jim Peterik. *Songwriting For Dummies*. Hoboken, N.J.: John Wiley & Sons, 2002. Written for the novice songwriter, this book will guide readers through the process of writing and producing their own original music—from conception to publication. How to write lyrics, find a publisher, and deal with music-industry professionals are covered.

Bartlett, Bruce, and Jenny Bartlett. *Practical Recording Techniques*. 4th ed. Burlington, Mass.: Focal Press, 2005. A step-by-step approach to professional audio recording. Ideal for novice recording professionals, this practical guidebook provides tips on how to set up your own recording studio, no matter what your budget.

Benward, Bruce, and Gary White. *Music in Theory and Practice*. 7th ed. Boston, Mass.: McGraw-Hill Humanities, 2003. This textbook for music students offers a comprehensive analysis and discussion of musical theory.

Bessler, Ian. *2006 Songwriter's Market*. 29th ed. Cincinnati, Ohio: Writers Digest Books, 2005. Providing all of the latest submission guidelines and up-to-date contacts for songwriters seeking publication, this annual resource publication also serves as a guidebook on how to market and sell your work.

Blair, Linda, and Paula Elliot (eds.). *Careers in Music Librarianship II: Traditions and Transitions*. Lanham,

Md.: Scarecrow Press, 2004. Examining the evolution of music librarianship is the emphasis of this resource book for students and industry professionals.

Blume, Jason. *Inside Songwriting: Getting to the Heart of Creativity*. New York, N.Y.: Watson-Guptill Publications, 2003. Written by a songwriter for aspiring songwriters, this book chronicles the creative process of composing your own music.

———. *6 Steps to Songwriting Success: Comprehensive Guide to Writing and Marketing Hit Songs*. New York, N.Y.: Watson-Guptill Publications, 1999. Breaking down the songwriting process into six manageable steps is heralded as this book's success. Readers will find numerous writing exercises, to-do checklists, and a valuable appendix of professional resources.

Braheny, John. *The Craft and Business of Songwriting*. 2nd ed. Cincinnati, Ohio: Writers Digest Books, 2001. Filled with anecdotes and advice from well-known contemporary songwriters and performers, this book gives a behind-the-scenes peak into the business of songwriting and the creative processes of its artists.

Crouch, Tanja L. *100 Careers in the Music Business*. Hauppauge, N.Y.: Barron's Educational Series, 2001. Providing an overview of how the industry works, this book highlights the major job categories within the industry, explaining how each individual contributes in his or her own way, while detailing their job responsibilities, education requirements, and job outlooks.

Davis, William, Kate Gfeller, and Michael Thaut. *An Introduction to Music Therapy: Theory and Practice*. 2nd ed. Boston, Mass.: McGraw-Hill Humanities, 1999. Offering a comprehensive introduction and overview of the field of music therapy, this textbook provides students a solid history of the field and of the varied types of populations that music therapists encounter in their work.

Fricke, Jim, Charlie Ahearn, and Experience Music Project. *Yes Yes Y'All: The Experience Music Project Oral History of Hip-Hop's First Decade*. Cambridge, Mass.: Da Capo Press, 2002. This book serves as a comprehensive and complete history of hip-hop music in America. The origins of the movement are traced from the early 1970s to recent years.

Gaskell, Ed. *Make Your Own Music Video*. San Francisco, Calif.: CMP Books, 2004. Anyone interested in breaking into music video production will find this book a helpful source of information. From choosing the right software, to dealing with band members, to the editing process, practical advice is offered on how to create professional-quality music videos.

Gaynor, Mitchell. *The Healing Power of Sound: Recovery From Life-Threatening Illness Using Sound, Voice, and Music*. Boston, Mass.: Shambhala Publications, 2002. This book, written by a medical doctor, details a non-traditional approach to healing—through therapy focused on sound.

Gerardi, Robert. *Opportunities in Music Careers*. Rev. ed. New York, N.Y.: McGraw Hill, 2002. This educational career guidebook examines various job opportunities in the field of music for anyone who would like to turn their interest in music into a professional career.

Gibson, Bill A. *The S.M.A.R.T. Guide to Digital Recording, Software, and Plug-Ins*. Boston, Mass.: ArtistPro Publishing, 2005. Explaining everything you need to know about modern digital recording, this book provides a practical and informative overview of the software and hardware necessary to create professional-quality recordings.

———. *The S.M.A.R.T. Guide to Mixing and Mastering Audio Recordings*. Boston, Mass.: ArtistPro Publishing, 2005. With technological advances making it increasingly easy for anyone to mix their own music, this guidebook provides the necessary information to help aspiring recording technicians mix and master audio recordings.

Goldberg, Justin. *The Ultimate Survival Guide for the New Music Industry: A Handbook for Hell*. Los Angeles, Calif.: Lone Eagle Publishing Company, 2004. Written by an industry veteran, this book contains the down-and-dirty details of what it takes to make it in today's cutthroat music industry. Included with the book is a CD-ROM directory of music industry contacts.

Grout, Donald, Claude Palisca, and Peter Burkholder. *A History of Western Music*. 7th ed. New York, N.Y.: W.W. Norton & Company, 2005. Provides a complete history of western composers of music from the earliest times to the present.

Hanser, Suzanne. *The New Music Therapist's Handbook*. 2nd ed. Boston, Mass.: Berklee Press, 2000. This reference book for music therapists and students details research and revelations in the field of music therapy.

Harcourt, Nic. *Music Lust: Recommended Listening for Every Mood, Moment, and Reason*. Seattle, Wash.: Sasquatch Books, 2005. With the radio industry dictating what we hear on the radio today, this publication provides an in-depth description of the best music in every genre that isn't getting airtime.

Hatschek, Keith. *How to Get a Job in the Music and Recording Industry*. Boston, Mass.: Berklee Press Publications, 2001. Containing interviews with industry professionals, listings of key trade organizations and publications, and networking and resume advice, this book helps serious job seekers land their first job in the industry.

Horowitz, Joseph. *Classical Music in America: A History of Its Rise and Fall*. New York, N.Y.: W. W. Norton, 2005. This comprehensive history of American classical music begins in the late 19th century and extends through modern times. Every aspect of the genre is traced—its composers, conductors, managers, entrepreneurs, critics, and more.

Kamp, David. *Music Business Handbook and Career Guide*. 8th ed. Thousand Oaks, Calif.: Sage Publications, 2005. This comprehensive guidebook provides an in-depth look into the music business and its career opportunities. The latest edition provides valuable insight into how technological advances are affecting and changing the business.

———. *The Rock Snob's Dictionary: An Essential Lexicon of Rockological Knowledge*. Thousand Oaks, Calif.: Sage Publications, 2005. This humorous book offers a fun, sarcastic, and informative view on what takes to become a "rock snob."

Keith, Michael C. *The Radio Station*. 6th ed. Burlington, Mass.: Focal Press, 2003. Providing a comprehensive introduction to the inner workings of a radio station, this textbook is appropriate for students who want to learn about everything from job opportunities in radio, to recent technological advances, to the latest governmental regulations. This guidebook provides a complete overview of the industry, with a focus on the everyday, behind-the-scenes goings on of a radio station.

Kingsbury, Paul, and Country Music Hall of Fame and Museum. *The Encyclopedia of Country Music: The Ultimate Guide to the Music*. New York, N.Y.: Oxford University Press, 2004. This comprehensive history of eight decades of country music in America includes historical and sociological essays on the genre.

Krasilovsky, William, and Sidney Shemel. *This Business of Music: The Definitive Guide to the Music Industry*. 9th ed. New York, N.Y.: Billboard Books, 2003. First published in 1964, this publication is a must-have for anyone working in the music business. The latest edition includes pertinent updates on financial and legal issues relating to new laws affecting the industry and the effects of technological advances.

Lanthrop, Tad. *This Business of Music Marketing and Promotion*. Rev. ed. New York, N.Y.: Billboard Books, 2003. Providing real-word examples, this comprehensive book outlines traditional marketing guidelines as well as the latest technological developments that influence the business of music marketing.

Leikin, Molly-Ann. *How to Be a Hit Songwriter: Polishing and Marketing Your Lyrics and Music*. Milwaukee, Wisc.: Hal Leonard Corporation, 2003. Serving as a resource for aspiring songwriters, this book takes the reader from idea conception to recorded hit. Unique to this publication is a chapter on marketing your music on the Internet.

Olsen, Keith. *A Music Producer's Thoughts to Create By*. Boston, Mass.: ArtistPro Publishing, 2005. A six-time Grammy award winner offers advice on how to adapt to the times and create professional, high-quality music that will also make money. Technical, creative, and business aspects of the industry are covered.

Passman, Donald S. *All You Need to Know About the Music Business.* 5th ed. New York, N.Y.: Simon & Schuster, 2003. Written by an entertainment lawyer, this book provides necessary information for creative artists who want to learn how to succeed in the music business. This book explains the business side of the industry to the creative artists whose livelihoods rest on making sound business decisions.

Peters, Jacqueline. *Music Therapy: An Introduction.* 2nd ed. Springfield, Ill.: Charles C. Thomas Publisher, 2000. Providing an overview of the history of the field of music therapy, this publication also discusses the nature of the evolving discipline and the varied populations that are helped with music therapy.

Phillips, Kenneth H. *Basic Techniques of Conducting.* New York, N.Y.: Oxford University Press, 1997. A textbook for those studying to become vocal or instrumental music teachers, this textbook emphasizes the importance of physical gestures in developing your own conducting style.

Savona, Anthony. *Console Confessions: The Great Music Producers in Their Own Words.* San Francisco, Calif.: Backbeat Books, 2005. Music production—through the eyes of industry celebrities and their personal accounts of how their music is created—is covered in this industry guidebook.

Schwartz, Daylle Deanna. *Start and Run Your Own Record Label.* New York, N.Y.: Billboard Books, 2003. This how-to book provides a practical explanation of how to start your own successful record label in today's highly competitive market.

Shaw, Russell, and Dave Mercer. *Caution! Music & Video Downloading: Your Guide to Legal, Safe, and Trouble-Free Downloads.* Hoboken, N.J.: Wiley, 2004. Anyone who is interested in learning more about downloading music and video will benefit from this publication's advice on how to safely and legally download from your computer—while avoiding risky viruses, other computer safety concerns, and legal issues.

Starr, Larry, and Christopher Alan Waterman. *American Popular Music: From Minstrelsy to MTV.* New York, N.Y.: Oxford University Press, 2002. This book aims to describe how an American social identity has been created through its popular music.

Ward, Geoffrey C., and Ken Burns. *Jazz: A History of America's Music.* New York, N.Y.: Knopf, 2000. Providing a comprehensive history of jazz music, and featuring more than 500 photographs, this book discusses the birth and movement of this uniquely American style of music. This book serves as a companion to Ken Burn's PBS documentary, *Jazz.*

Wixen, Randall. *The Plain and Simple Guide to Music Publishing.* Milwaukee, Wisc.: Hal Leonard Corporation, 2005. Written by a music executive, this publication offers advice to industry professionals and musicians who want to learn how to successfully shape their careers in music publishing.

❏ PERIODICALS

American Music Teacher. Published bimonthly (Music Teachers National Association, 441 Vine Street, Suite 505, Cincinnati, Ohio 45202-2811, 888-512-5278, mtnanet@mtna.org, http://www.mtna.org/amt.htm), this publication will help music teachers stay abreast of the latest trends and educational issues that affect their classrooms. Readers will discover forums for expressing their own concerns along with news updates, feature stories, and listings of music conferences and activities for both personal and student professional growth.

The American Organist. Published monthly (American Guild of Organists, 475 Riverside Drive, Suite 1260, New York, N.Y. 10115-0055, 800-AGO-5115, members@agohq.org, http://www.agohq.org/tao/index.html). Devoted entirely to organ and choral music, this publication is the most widely read publication of its kind in the world.

American Songwriter. Published bimonthly (1303 16th Avenue South, 2nd Floor, Nashville, Tenn. 37212-2929, 615-321-6096, info@americansongwriter.com, http://www.americansongwriter.com). Professional and aspiring songwriters will find this consumer publication of particular interest, with its coverage of both the artistic and business sides of the songwriting industry. Each issue contains interviews with up-and-coming songwriters, publishing executives, legendary songwriters, music produc-ers, and other industry professionals. Subscriptions to the hard-copy publication come with full access to the Web site content as well.

Billboard. Published weekly (Subscriptions, PO Box 15158, North Hollywood, Calif. 91615-5158, 800-562-2706, billboard@espcomp.com, http://www.billboard.com), this well-known publication, best known for its ratings charts, provides the latest news and reviews in the music industry. Subscribers receive full online access as well as the print publication. Besides covering the latest chart-topping hits and artists, the publication also provides the latest updates on the touring scene, industry classified ads, and directories.

Blender. Published monthly by Dennis Publishing (1040 Avenue of the Americas, New York, N.Y. 10018-3703, 212-302-2626, http://www.blender.com/in_print), this self-proclaimed "ultimate guide to music and more" is the most recent addition to the list of consumer general-interest music magazines. From the publishers of *Maxim* and *Stuff,* this magazine targets a youthful audience of popular music fans. Issues contain feature stories on popular bands, news updates, reviews, tours and ticket information, and more.

CMJ New Music Monthly. Published monthly (CMJ Network, 151 West 25th Street, 12th Floor, New York, N.Y. 10001-7204, 917-606-1908, http://www.cmj.com). With a focus on non-commercial new music, this consumer magazine not only contains feature stories on emerging artists, but each issue also comes with a CD sampler.

ComposerUSA. Published quarterly by the National Association of Composers (PO Box 49256, Barrington Station, Los Angeles, Calif. 90049-0256, 318-357-0924, nacusa@music-usa.org, http://www.music-usa.org/nacusa), this membership publication contains listings of upcoming member performances, recordings, broadcasts, commissions, and awards. Performance reviews and opportunities are also highlighted.

Conductor Opportunities Bulletin. Published monthly (5300 Glenside Drive, Suite 2207, Richmond, Va. 23228-3938, 804-553-1378, publications@conductorsguild.org, http://www.conductorsguild.org/main.asp?pageID=29). Providing important job vacancies, workshops, and study opportunities both in the United States and abroad for anyone working in the conducting/orchestral industry, this is a must-have publication for those seeking career advancement or professional development.

Dirty Linen. Published bimonthly (18 ½ Cedar Avenue, Baltimore, Md. 21286-7843, 410-583-7973, subscribe@dirtylinen.com, http://www.dirtylinen.com). With a focus on folk and world music, this consumer magazine is full of all kinds of reviews—concerts, books, videos, and recordings—as well as feature stories and news updates.

Downbeat. Published monthly (P.O. Box 906 Elmhurst, Ill. 60126-0906, 800-554-7470, http://www.downbeat.com). Jazz music—past and present—is the focus of this consumer publication. Each issue contains articles on featured artists, reviews, music news, and more.

EQ. Published monthly by CMP Entertainment Media (2800 Campus Drive, San Mateo, Calif. 94403-2506, 888-266-5828, eqmag@sfsdayton.com, http://www.eqmag.com), this publication for recording industry engineers contains feature articles that profile industry leaders, equipment and gadget reviews, monthly columns, and more. With content that is technical in nature, readers will find themselves educated and well informed on industry standards and emerging technology.

General Music Today. Published three times yearly by MENC: National Association for Music Education (1806 Robert Fulton Drive, Reston, Va. 20191-5462, 800-336-3768, elizabethp@menc.org, http://www.menc.org/publication/articles/journals.html), this online-only journal offers practical and applicable ideas for music educators at all levels to implement in their classrooms.

International Musician. Published monthly (American Federation of Musicians, New York Headquarters, 1501 Broadway, Suite 600, New York, N.Y. 10136-5505, 212-869-1330, http://www.afm.org/public/home/index.php), this unique magazine for musicians contains articles pertaining to real-world issues for those working in the music industry. You'll find career articles, features about technology and legislative issues, and much more. Articles cover all types of music—from symphonic to rock—and do not focus on celebrities.

Journal of Music Teacher Education. Published biannually by MENC: National Association for Music Education (1806 Robert Fulton Drive, Reston, Va. 20191-5462, 800-336-3768, teresap@menc.org, http://www.menc.org/publication/articles/journals.html). Offered in an online-only format, this scholarly publication targets educators in higher education who are training students to become music educators. You'll find curriculum guidelines, current theory on teaching methods, and more in this journal.

Journal of Music Therapy. Published quarterly (American Music Therapy Association, 8455 Colesville Road, Suite 1000, Silver Spring, Md. 20910-3392, 301-589-3300, http://www.musictherapy.org/products/pubs.html), this scholarly journal contains reports and essays highlighting the latest research findings in the industry. The journal targets an audience of professionals who are interested in current theory that is being explored as well as publications that are being written to advance the field.

Journal of Research in Music Education. Published quarterly by MENC: National Association for Music Education (1806 Robert Fulton Drive, Reston, Va. 20191-5462, 800-336-3768, ellaw@menc.org, http://www.

menc.org/publication/articles/journals.html), this research journal for music educators contains scholarly articles on music theory and the latest reports regarding musical projects and research being conducted by scholars in the field.

Journal of the Audio Engineering Society. Published monthly by the Audio Engineering Society (60 East 42nd Street, Room 2520, New York, N.Y. 10165-2520, 212-661-8528, http://www.aes.org/journal). Devoted exclusively to audio technology, this peer-reviewed journal contains the latest industry reports, society and product development news, and trade convention schedules.

Journal of the Conductors Guild. Published semi-annually by the Conductors Guild (5300 Glenside Drive, Suite 2207, Richmond, Va. 23228-3938, 804-553-1378, publications@conductorsguild.org, http://www.conductorsguild.org/main.asp?pageID=26), this scholarly publication for conductors contains book reviews, transcripts of important conferences, articles about the craft or history of conducting, and other academic topics relating to musical scores and orchestral arrangements.

Mix Magazine. Published monthly by Prism Business Media (6400 Hollis, #12, Emeryville, Calif. 94608-1086, 510-653-3307, mix@espcomp.com, http://mixonline.com). Professional audio and music producers are the prime audience for this leading trade publication. Featuring articles on technical subjects, new product announcements and equipment reviews, industry news and profiles, and more, this publication covers a wide range of topics in addition to publishing a yearly *Mix Master Directory* of recording studios and audio/visual facilities.

Music & Entertainment Industry Educators Association Journal. Published annually by the Music & Entertainment Industry Educators Association (1900 Belmont Boulevard, Nashville, Tenn. 37212-3757, 615-460-6946, office@meiea.org, http://www.meiea.org/Journals.html), this scholarly journal highlights significant issues that affect all segments of the music and entertainment industry.

Music Educators Journal. Published five times yearly by MENC: National Association for Music Education (1806 Robert Fulton Drive, Reston, Va. 20191-5462, 800-336-3768, teresap@menc.org, http://www.menc.org/publication/articles/journals.html). Containing essays on educational philosophies and musical education teaching methods, this scholarly publication also includes articles that detail the latest trends, issues, products, and services of relevance to music educators.

Music Therapy Perspectives. Published biannually by the American Music Therapy Association (8455 Colesville Road, Suite 1000, Silver Spring, Md. 20910-3392, 301-589-3300, http://www.musictherapy.org/products/pubs.html), this professional journal of the American Music Therapy Association targets a wide audience of industry insiders, outsiders, and educators. Readers will find articles that discuss the practice of music therapy in easy-to-understand language that is accessible to everyone.

Podium Notes. Published quarterly by the Conductors Guild (5300 Glenside Drive, Suite 2207, Richmond, Va. 23228-3938, 804-553-1378, publications@conductorsguild.org, http://www.conductorsguild.org/main.asp?pageID=27). This official newsletter of the Conductors Guild contains articles on guild activities, commentary from organization leaders, book reviews, important happenings in the field, and more.

Pro Sound News. Published by CMP Entertainment Media (460 Park Avenue South, 9th Floor, New York, N.Y. 10016-7315, 212-378-0400, http://www.prosoundnews.com). Featuring headline news, product spotlights, and an industry calendar, this publication, free to industry insiders, covers topics of importance to those working in audio production. On the publication's Web site, students will find a complete directory of educational degree and certificate programs in audio technology that are available in the United States.

Radio & Records. Published weekly (2049 Century Park East, 41st Floor, Los Angeles, Calif. 90067-3101, 310-553-4330, subscribe@

radioandrecords.com, http://www.
radioandrecords.com). Containing
the latest ratings, news, and format
updates, this industry publication
provides articles and news of interest
to industry insiders. The publication
is available by subscription and can
be packaged in varying combinations
with additional daily or weekly news
e-mail or fax updates.

Remix. Published monthly (PO Box 349,
Mt. Morris, Ill. 61054-0349, 800-275-
1989, remx@kable.com, http://www.
remixmag.com). With each issue containing feature stories and tech sector
articles, this publication is for anyone
producing electronic music—from DJs
to producers, engineers to performers.
This consumer publication focuses on
hardware, software, and equipment
necessary to produce today's urban
and electronic music.

Rolling Stone. Published biweekly (1290
Avenue of the Americas, New York,
N.Y. 10104-0298, 212-484-1616,
http://www.rollingstone.com). Known
as the consumer publication focusing on popular music, this magazine
provides the latest musical artist news
and reviews along with movie reviews,
entertainment news, political commentary, and feature articles. Sample
articles can be read online.

Spin. Published monthly (205 Lexington
Avenue, New York, N.Y. 10016-6022,
212-231-7400, http://www.spin.com).
Covering the latest in popular music,
this publication contains feature
articles, news updates, music reviews

and much more. The publication's
content is targeted to a youthful and
hip audience.

Teaching Music. Published five times
yearly by MENC: National Association for Music Education (1806 Robert
Fulton Drive, Reston, Va. 20191-5462,
800-336-3768, elizabethp@menc.org,
http://www.menc.org/publication/
articles/journals.html). With articles of
interest to music teachers, each issue
of this publication addresses practical issues that music educators face in
their careers. Advocacy resources and
how-to articles make this publication
particularly relevant to beginning professionals who are seeking advice from
industry veterans.

Update. Published biannually by
MENC: National Association for
Music Education (1806 Robert Fulton Drive, Reston, Va. 20191-5462,
800-336-3768, dorothyw@menc.
org, http://www.menc.org/publica-
tion/articles/journals.html), this
online-only publication gives music
educators practical advice on how to
implement the latest research findings in their everyday classroom
activities.

Vibe. Published monthly (215 Lexington
Avenue, New York, N.Y. 10016-6023,
212-448-7300, http://www.vibe.com),
this publication claims to cover everything that is "born of urban music."
This includes celebrity and music
news, fashion, lifestyle, sports, and
more. Appealing to a young and mul-
ticultural audience, this publication

serves as an authoritative resource on everything relating to pop culture.

The Woman Conductor. Published three times annually by the Women Band Directors National Association (296 Dailey Hill Circle, Ringgold, Ga. 30736-8156, http://www.womenband directors.org), this magazine features updates on association happenings and details opportunities for women in conducting.

Surf the Web

You must use the Internet to do research and to explore. The Internet is the closest you'll get to what's happening right now all around the world. This chapter gets you started with an annotated list of Web sites related to music. Try a few. Follow the links. Maybe even venture as far as asking questions in a chat room. The more you read about and interact with music personnel, the better prepared you'll be when you're old enough to participate as a professional.

One caveat: you probably already know that URLs change all the time. If a Web address listed below is out of date, try searching on the site's name or other key words. Chances are if it's still out there, you'll find it. If it's not, maybe you'll find something better!

About.com: Music 101
http://musiced.about.com/
    od/beginnersguide/a/intro.
    htm?terms=music

About.com tells you everything you always wanted to know "about" any given subject: in this case—music education. You'll find sections on the history of musical genres, timelines, music theory, online music lessons, schools, a glossary of music terms, links to free resources, and more. If you're looking for musical instruments or products of any kind, there are plenty of links to online retailers. Articles on the home page range in topic—you might find stories about famous female composers during women's history month or features on specific instruments. Job seekers can also access a job database of music-related positions across the country. The "forums" section is a great place to discuss music topics with like-minded individuals and find answers to questions about music.

AllMusic
http://www.allmusic.com

Music lovers will find this to be a unique Web site, covering a vast array of musical genres without being overwhelming in its attempt to do so. You'll find separate pages for new releases (of every kind of music), classical reviews, editors' choice, and writers' block. Editors' Choice is a great section to check out if you are interested in a musical genre but don't know a lot about its emerging artists. The editors of the Web site give their picks of the best new music, which is a good place to start. The Writers' Block section might help you determine whose opinions you think you'll value most. This section essentially provides a musical biography of each of the staff writers. Another feature allows you to explore music by genre, mood, theme, country, and instrument.

AllMusic also publishes books about each genre of music, and you'll find links to purchase these books through an online bookseller.

American Federation of Musicians: Music Schools Search

http://www.afm.org/public/ musicians/schools.php

The American Federation of Musicians is a union designed to help protect musicians' professional interests. The music schools search is an excellent tool to aid in your search for the perfect music school for you. Searching by state or country, you are given a listing of corresponding links to music schools or universities with well-known music departments. This serves as an excellent starting point for high school students who think they want to major in music. On the right-hand side of the page you'll also find links to scholarship opportunities for musicians, job postings, and reputable booking agents.

American Society of Composers, Authors, and Publishers

http://www.ascap.com/index.html

This professional association's Web site serves as a resource center for anyone who is working, or hoping to find work, as a professional musician. The main page highlights the most recent top stories and news releases in the music spotlight. Along the left-hand column of the page, you'll find sections titled Career Development and Inside Music. Inside Music takes you to top stories of the day in a variety of categories: audio portraits, concert music, film and television, Nashville, musical theatre, pop/rock, jazz, and rhythm and soul. Each of these has links to pertinent information in each category. For example, on the musical theatre page not only will you find feature articles in the category, but you'll also find links to scholarships in musical theatre and musical theatre workshops in cities across the United States. The Career Development section is subcategorized into articles and advice, collaborator corner, an events calendar, resource guide, and workshops.

Billboard

http://www.billboard.com/bbcom/ index.jsp

This Web site of the well-known magazine known for its ratings charts covers the latest in popular music. You'll find sections devoted to the latest charts, news and reviews, artists, shopping, industry resources (directories, classifieds), entertainment, and online chatting. Download the hottest new ring tones, find out what happened on this day in music 10 years ago, and discover which songs and artists were topping the charts last year and more. You may also choose to subscribe to *Billboard*'s e-mail newsletter or check out the latest new CD releases (along with reviews).

GetSigned.com

http://www.getsigned.com

Aspiring musicians or music industry professionals should visit this Web site to discover a lot of really practical and essential advice. The site claims to be "the number-one resource for getting signed, music marketing, record deal information, and more." And it really does seem to back up its claim. You'll find articles written by lawyers and industry experts who don't hesitate to tell the truth—it's not as easy as it looks to get into this business. Additional sections cover music law, music promotion, managing bands, lessons, recording, news, and more. Particularly useful are the e-book downloads with titles such as *The Musicians Guide to Pursing a Major Record Deal.* Downloadable as PDF files, these contain a wealth of valuable information.

MTV
http://www.mtv.com

This Web site of the famed music video television station encompasses a range of pop culture topics of interest to teens—videos, music, television, movies, games, style, and more. News features highlight the most up-to-date happenings in these categories. You'll also find message boards, shopping, and mobile features (ring tones, alerts, games, and more). Pop culture junkies will find this Web site a must-bookmark page.

National Academy of Recording Arts and Sciences
http://www.grammy.org

The National Academy of Recording Arts and Sciences, the official presenter of the Grammy Awards, maintains a mission to "advance artistic and technical excellence, work to ensure a vital and free creative environment, and act as an advocate on behalf of music and its makers." Industry insiders and fans alike will enjoy this Web site, which is full of information about the Academy as well as its most important night—the Grammy Awards. Download nominated albums, view winners lists, or check out what your favorite stars were wearing. View video clips of live performances at the Grammys, and read press releases of the night's biggest events. You'll also find information about the Grammy Foundation and Musicares, which are branches that work to promote music awareness and charitable giving. Individuals in the music business can even download an application and discover how to apply for membership in the academy so that you can become a part of the Grammy nomination process yourself!

National Association of Schools of Music
http://nasm.arts-accredit.org

If you are looking for a music school to attend—whether it be a conservatory or a college or university program—this Web site is essential to your research process. This association establishes national standards for schools and grants accreditation based on a school's ability to meet a certain level of excellence. The Frequently Asked Questions: Students, Parents, Public section will be most beneficial to students looking for the perfect music school. Here you will discover a complete list of the 610 accredited music schools along with guidelines on how to go about finding the best school to fit your needs. Information about scholarships and grants, school admissions processes, types of degree programs, and much more is also discussed. Discover how to prepare for an audition, when and how to apply for financial aid, and what levels of giftedness are necessary to attain professional success in different areas of this field. Useful publications are also available for download from the Web site as well. One such example is a publication titled, *Giftedness, Arts Study, and Work.*

PBS: Arts & Drama: Music
http://www.pbs.org/arts/arts_music. html

Some of the best footage of live musical performances and video biographies is produced for air on PBS. This Web site gives you access to information about these programs that have recently aired or are available for purchase through PBS membership. You'll find categories including American Masters, Great Performances, Frontline/World, Soundstage (contemporary and classic rock/pop), On Stage at the Kennedy Center, and more. Each link takes you to more in-depth information about the performer or performance and how you can view it (either on television or on video). Under American Masters, for instance, you can click on Bob Marley, where you'll be taken to a page that includes a feature essay, career timeline, and filmmaker interview as well as links to additional related Web sites.

Recording Industry Association of America
http://www.riaa.com/default.asp

According to this association's Web site, the music business is a $40 billion a year industry, and sales in the United States account for one third of that amount. The Recording Industry Association of America is the trade organization that serves its members in such a way that the music industry maintains its creative and financial viability in today's business environment. On this Web site you'll find extensive news releases covering every aspect of the business, information on industry issues, and current research and data. You'll also find links to legal cases, facts and figures, marketing reports, consumer trends, and more. If you are interested in working in the music industry, in any capacity—from musician to record industry executive—you'll benefit from reading the information presented on this highly informative Web site. You may also want to look into becoming a member of the organization.

Songfacts
http://www.songfacts.com

This fun Web site will be particularly interesting to trivia buffs or to anyone interested in learning about a favorite song or artist. You'll find a massive searchable database full of information compiled by music lovers, and all you have to do to access it is register (membership is free). The database provides information about albums, the years that individual songs were released, their highest chart positions, and interesting facts about each song and artist. If you ever wondered about the meaning of a particular song's lyrics, this is the Web site to check out. The message boards contain further answers to any question you might have and provide an excellent forum to pose any song- or artist-related question.

Sun Studio

http://www.sunstudio.com/index.html

Sun Studio is known as the "birthplace of rock 'n' roll," and this Web site is dedicated to telling you a little more about this historical spot. You can listen to an audio presentation about artists like Elvis, Jerry Lee Lewis, Carl Perkins, and Johnny Cash, all of whom made this recording studio into the historic place that it is. You may also sign up to receive the company's e-zine by e-mail.

This Day in Music

http://www.thisdayinmusic.com/index.php

This trivia Web site tells you just what it says it will and more. Find out what happened on any certain day in the world of music—which songs were in the top spot each year or who was born on your birthday. Discover which album your favorite artists say was the first album they owned. Read interesting and ironic quotes of the day. Find "best of" lists, jokes, games, and much more.

Women in Music National Network: Careers in Music

http://www.womeninmusic.com/Careers.htm

Visit this Web site to preview music business occupations. You'll discover categories in performance, songwriting, music production and engineering, film scoring, contemporary writing/jazz composition, music education, music therapy, music business management, tours/road work, record companies, and other miscellaneous positions. Each of these is further broken down into specific positions, or job titles, and given a brief description. Students who are beginning to research opportunities in the industry will find this Web site to be a good starting point. You can also access job postings for a small fee.

Yahoo: Entertainment: Music

http://dir.yahoo.com/Entertainment/Music

This popular search engine divides music into four top categories (artists, regions, genres, and instruments) along with a variety of smaller categories. With an enormous range of listings in the major categories, weeding through the results may be overwhelming. The smaller categories, however, may provide very relevant links to information you are seeking. Sample categories include reference, recording, musicology, music Web logs, music industry resources, and more. Yahoo lists these categories as having a more manageable number of links (less than 100), making it much easier to discover relevant sources of information in a subject matter of choice.

Young Composers

http://www.youngcomposers.com

Musicians of all ages and experience levels will find this forum an excellent place to obtain feedback from their peers and to learn more about all aspects of the music industry. With an emphasis on

classical music of the 18th and 19th centuries, this Web site strives to encourage
creative individuals to write and record
music that goes beyond what is popular in
contemporary society. You can create and
post your own profile on the site, share
your music with others, and gain important feedback. Visitors can also engage in
online chats or message-board conversa-
tions with like-minded individuals, and
learn about how to have their work pro-
fessionally recorded.

Ask for Money

By the time most students get around to thinking about applying for scholarships, grants, and other financial aid, they have already extolled their personal, academic, and creative virtues to such lengths in essays, interviews, and audio portfolios for college applications that even their own grandmothers wouldn't recognize them. The thought of filling out yet another application fills students with dread. And why bother? Won't the same five or six kids who have been competing for academic and artistic honors for years walk away with all the really good scholarships?

The truth is, most of the scholarships available to high school and college students are being offered because an organization wants to promote interest in a particular field, encourage more students to become qualified to enter it, and help those students afford an education. Certainly, having a great grade point average is a valuable asset. More often than not, however, grade point averages aren't even mentioned; the focus is on the area of interest and what a student has done to distinguish himself or herself in that area. In fact, sometimes the only requirement is that the scholarship applicant must be studying in a particular area.

❑ GUIDELINES

When applying for scholarships, there are a few simple guidelines that can help ease the process considerably.

Plan Ahead

The absolute worst thing you can do is wait until the last minute. Keep in mind that obtaining recommendations or other supporting data in time to meet an application deadline is incredibly difficult. And no one does his or her best thinking or writing under pressure. So get off to a good start by reviewing scholarship applications as early as possible—months, even a year, in advance. If the current scholarship information isn't available, ask for a copy of last year's version. Once you have the scholarship information or application in hand, give it a thorough read. Try to determine how your experience or situation best fits into the scholarship, or if it even fits at all. Don't waste your time applying for a scholarship in literature if you couldn't finish *Great Expectations*.

If possible, research the award or scholarship, including past recipients and, where applicable, the person in whose name the scholarship is offered. Often, scholarships are established to memorialize an individual who majored in music, for example, but in other cases, the scholarship is to memorialize the *work* of an individual. In those cases, try to get a feel for the spirit of the person's work. If you have any similar interests, experiences, or abilities, don't hesitate to mention these.

Talk to others who received the scholarship, or to students currently studying in the same area or field of interest in which the scholarship is offered, and try to gain insight into possible applications or work related to that field. When you're working on the essay asking why you want this scholarship, you'll have real answers—"I would benefit from receiving this scholarship because studying music therapy will help me to improve the lives of people with physical, mental, or emotional disabilities."

Take your time writing the essays. Make sure you are answering the question or questions on the application and not merely restating facts about yourself. Don't be afraid to get creative; try to imagine what you would think of if you had to sift through hundreds of applications: What would you want to know about the candidate? What would convince you that someone was deserving of the scholarship? Work through several drafts and have someone whose advice you respect—a parent, teacher, or guidance counselor—review the essay for grammar and content.

Finally, if you know in advance which scholarships you want to apply for, there might still be time to stack the deck in your favor by getting an internship, volunteering, or working part time. Bottom line: the more you know about a scholarship and the sooner you learn it, the better.

Follow Directions

Think of it this way: many of the organizations that offer scholarships devote 99.9 percent of their time to something other than the scholarship for which you are applying. Don't make a nuisance of yourself by pestering them for information. Simply follow the directions as they are presented to you. If the scholarship application specifies that you write for further information, then write for it—don't call.

Pay close attention to whether you're applying for an award, a scholarship, a prize, or financial aid. Often these words are used interchangeably, but just as often they have different meanings. An award is usually given for something you have done: built a park or helped distribute meals to the elderly; or something you have created: a musical composition, a design, an essay, a short film, a screenplay, or an invention. On the other hand, a scholarship is frequently a renewable sum of money that is given to a person to help defray the costs of college. Scholarships are given to candidates who meet the necessary criteria based on musical talent, essays, eligibility, grades, or sometimes all four.

Supply all the necessary documents, information, and fees, and make the deadlines. You won't win any scholarships by forgetting to include a recommendation from a teacher or failing to postmark the application by the deadline. Get it right the first time, and get it done on time.

Apply Early

Once you have the application in hand, don't dawdle. If you've requested it far enough in advance, there shouldn't be any reason for you not to turn it in well in advance of the deadline. You never know, if it comes down to two candidates, your timeliness just might be the deciding factor!

Be Yourself

Don't make promises you can't keep. There are plenty of hefty scholarships available, but if they all require you to study something that you don't enjoy, you'll be miserable in college. And the side effects from switching majors after you've accepted a scholarship could be even worse. Be yourself.

Don't Limit Yourself

There are many sources for scholarships, beginning with your guidance counselor and ending with the Internet. All of the search engines have education categories. Start there and search by keywords, such as "financial aid," "scholarship," and "award." And go beyond the scholarships listed in these pages.

If you know of an organization related to or involved with the field of your choice, write a letter asking if they offer scholarships. If they don't offer scholarships, don't stop there. Write them another letter, or better yet, schedule a meeting with the president or someone in the public relations office and ask if they would be willing to sponsor a scholarship for you. Of course, you'll need to prepare yourself well for such a meeting because you're selling a priceless commodity—yourself. Be confident. Tell them all about yourself, what you want to study and why, and

let them know what you would be willing to do in exchange—volunteer at their favorite charity, write up reports on your progress in school, or work part-time on school breaks, full-time during the summer. Explain why you're a wise investment. The sky's the limit!

❏ THE LIST

Academy of Television Arts and Sciences

5220 Lankershim Boulevard
North Hollywood, CA 91601-3109
818-754-2800
http://www.emmys.org/foundation/
collegetvawards.php

The academy offers the College Television Awards and the Fred Rogers Memorial Scholarship.

The College Television Awards competition rewards excellence in college (undergraduate and graduate) student film/video productions in the following categories: animation: non-traditional (computer-generated); animation: traditional; children's programs; comedy; documentary; drama; magazine shows; music programs; and newscasts. All entries must have been made for college course credit between September 1 and December 15 to qualify. Entries longer than one hour will not be accepted. News, sports, and magazine shows, children's, and comedy entries must not exceed 30 minutes. Entries can be submitted on Beta, Beta SP, DVD, or VHS video. First place winners receive $2,000; second place winners, $1,000; and third place winners $500.

College students who are pursuing degrees in early childhood education, child development/child psychology, film/television production, media arts, music, or animation may apply for the $10,000 Fred Rogers Memorial Scholarship. Applicants must have the ultimate goal of working in the field of children's media. Particular attention will be given to student applicants from inner city or rural communities.

Broadcast Education Association (BEA)

1771 N Street, NW
Washington, DC 20036-2891
888-380-7222
beainfo@beaweb.org
http://www.beaweb.org

An association of university broadcasting faculty, industry professionals, and graduate students, BEA offers more than 10 annual scholarships (ranging from $1,250 to $5,000) in broadcasting for college students. Applicants must be able to demonstrate superior academic performance and a dedication to a career in broadcasting.

Collegeboard.com

http://apps.collegeboard.com/
cbsearch_ss/welcome.jsp

This testing service (PSAT, SAT, etc.) also offers a scholarship search engine at its Web site. It features scholarships (not all music-related) worth nearly $3 billion. You can search by specific major (such as music, music management, and performing arts) and a variety of other criteria.

CollegeNET

http://www.collegenet.com

CollegeNET features 600,000 scholarships (not all music-related) worth more than $1.6 billion. You can search by keyword (such as "music," "music education," and "performing arts") or by creating a personality profile of your interests.

Connecticut Association of Schools/Connecticut Interscholastic Athletic Conference

Attn: Dr. Robert F. Carroll
30 Realty Drive
Cheshire, CT 06410-1655
203-250-1111
http://www.casciac.org/hsawards.shtml

Connecticut high school graduating seniors who are accepted into a college degree program in the performing arts may apply for the Bruce Eagleson Memorial Scholarship. Applicants must have graduated from a Connecticut high school, have demonstrated involvement showcasing their artistic work in performances, be committed to community and public service, and show financial need. One award of $10,000 and two awards of $5,000 are provided. Visit the association's Web site to download an application.

Daughters of the American Revolution (DAR)

Attn: Scholarship Committee
1776 D Street, NW
Washington, DC 20006-5303
202-628-1776
http://www.dar.org/natsociety/
edout_scholar.cfm

General scholarships are available to female students who have been accepted by or who are currently enrolled in a college or university in the United States. Selection criteria include academic excellence, commitment to field of study, and financial need; applicants need not be affiliated with DAR. A scholarship program is also available for Native American students. Contact the Scholarship Committee for more information.

FastWeb

http://fastweb.monster.com

FastWeb is one of the best-known scholarship search engines around. It features 1.3 million scholarships (not all music-related) worth more than $3 billion. To use this resource, you will need to register (free).

Florida State Music Teachers Association (FSMTA)

Attn: Gloria Bolivar, VP Competitive Events
13202 Dorchester Drive
Seminole, FL 33776-3111
727-397-1771
http://www.fmta.org/awards.html

Florida high school seniors and college students with expertise in musical performance may apply for a variety of scholarships and awards from the association. Awards range from $50 to $600. Applicants should contact their local music teachers or the FSMTA for additional information on eligibility requirements.

Foundation for the Carolinas

217 South Tryon Street
Charlotte, NC 28201-3201

704-973-4500
infor@fftc.org
http://www.fftc.org

The foundation administers more than 70 scholarship funds that offer awards to undergraduate and graduate students pursuing study in the arts, business, education, and other disciplines. Visit its Web site for a searchable list of awards.

Glenn Miller Birthplace Society

107 East Main Street, PO Box 61
Clarinda, IA 51632-2110
712-542-2461
caldrich@clarinda.k12.ia.us
http://www.glennmiller.org/scholar.htm

Graduating high school seniors and first-year college students who intend to major in music in college and pursue some form of musical career may apply for the Glenn Miller Scholarship Competition. Awards of $3,000, $2,000, and $1,000 are provided to competition winners. Visit the society's Web site for additional information on the application and competition.

Golden Key International Honor Society

621 North Avenue, NE, Suite C-100
Atlanta, GA 30308-2857
800-377-2401
http://www.goldenkey.org

Golden Key is an academic honor society that offers its members "opportunities for individual growth through leadership, career development, networking, and service." It awards more than $400,000 in scholarships annually through 17 different award programs. Membership in the society is selective; only the top 15 percent of college juniors and seniors—who may be pursuing education in any college major—are considered for membership by the organization. There is a one-time membership fee of $60 to $65. Contact the society for more information.

GuaranteedScholarships.com
http://www.guaranteed-scholarships. com

This Web site offers lists (by college) of scholarships, grants, and financial aid (not all music-related) that "require no interview, essay, portfolio, audition, competition, or other secondary requirement."

Hawaii Community Foundation
1164 Bishop Street, Suite 800
Honolulu, HI 96813-2810
808-537-633scholarships@
    hcf-hawaii.org
http://www.hawaiicommunityfoundation.
    org/scholar/scholar.php

The foundation offers a variety of scholarships for high school seniors and college students planning to study or currently studying music, business, education, and other majors in college. Applicants must be residents of Hawaii, demonstrate financial need, and plan to attend a two- or four-year college. Visit the foundation's Web site for more information and to apply online.

Hispanic College Fund (HCF)
1717 Pennsylvania Avenue, NW,
    Suite 460
Washington, DC 20006-2614
800-644-4223
hcf-info@hispanicfund.org
http://www.hispanicfund.org

The Hispanic College Fund, in collaboration with several major corporations, offers many scholarships for high school seniors and college students planning to study or currently attending college. Applicants must be Hispanic, live in the United States or Puerto Rico, and have a GPA of at least 3.0 on a 4.0 scale. Contact the HCF for more information.

Illinois Career Resource Network
http://www.ilworkinfo.com/icrn.htm

Created by the Illinois Department of Employment Security, this useful site offers a great scholarship search engine, as well as detailed information on careers (including those in music and the performing arts). You can search for music scholarships based on majors (such as music business and management, music composition and theory, music history, music teacher education, music therapy, musical instrument repair, and musicology and ethnomusicology), and other criterion. This site is available to everyone, not just Illinois residents; you can get a password by simply visiting the site. The Illinois Career Information System is just one example of sites created by state departments of employment security (or departments of labor) to assist students with financial- and career-related issues. After checking out this site, visit your state's department of labor Web site to see what it offers.

Mix Foundation for Excellence in Audio

TEC Awards Scholarship
1547 Palos Verdes Mall, #294
Walnut Creek, CA 94597-2228
925-939-6149
http://www.mixfoundation.org

College students who are currently pursuing study in audio or other media communications arts may apply for scholarships from the foundation. Applicants must have a GPA of at least 3.5 and be enrolled full time. Contact the foundation for more information.

National Association of Pastoral Musicians (NPM)

NPM Scholarships
962 Wayne Avenue, Suite 210
Silver Spring, MD 20910-4461
240-247-3000
npmsing@npm.org
http://www.npm.org/Membership/
   scholarship.htm

College students who are enrolled in a degree program related to pastoral music, intend to work as pastoral musicians for at least two years, and demonstrate financial need may apply for academic scholarships. Applicants must also be members of the NPM. Awards range from $500 to $4,500. Visit the association's Web site for further information about the many scholarships that are awarded.

National Endowment for the Arts (NEA)

1100 Pennsylvania Avenue, NW
Washington, DC 20004-2501
202-682-5400
http://arts.endow.gov/grants

The NEA, which was established by Congress in 1965 to support excellence in the arts, offers grants to musicians and arts organizations. Visit the NEA's Web site for a detailed list of available programs.

National Opera Association (NOA)

Vocal Competition
PO Box 60869
Canyon, TX 79016-0869
806-651-2857
rhansen@mail.wtamu.edu
http://www.noa.org

Young opera singers between the ages of 18 and 24 may enter the association's vocal competition. Applicants must be currently enrolled undergraduate students, have a teacher or opera director who is a member of the NOA, and attend an institution that is a NOA member. Awards range from $500 to $2,000. Visit the association's Web site to download an application and to obtain further contest details.

Oregon Music Teachers Association

Attn: Victoria Buhn, Education
   Chair
2100 Ridgeway Drive
Eugene, OR 97401-1724
541-683-5231
virginiabuhn@earthlink.net
http://www.oregonmta.org/Forms.html

The association offers a variety of performance-based competitions for

Oregon high school students and young adults. It also offers one non-performance based scholarships for Oregon high school students. Visit the association's Web site for details.

Sallie Mae
http://www.collegeanswer.com/
   paying/scholarship_search/pay_
   scholarship_search.jsp

This Web site offers a scholarship database of more than 2.4 million awards (not all music-related) worth more than $15 billion. You must register (free) to use the database.

Salute to Education Inc.
PO Box 833425
Miami, FL 33283-3425
305-476-7709
steinfo@stescholarships.org
http://www.stescholarships.org/SC_
   categories.html#7

Graduating high school seniors who attend a Miami-Dade or Broward County, Florida, high school and who also reside in one of these counties may apply for the $1,000 Salute to Education Performing Arts Scholarship. Applicants must also be legal residents of the United States, have a minimum weighted GPA of 3.0, demonstrate a commitment to service by participating in at least one school or community organization, and intend to pursue a college degree at an accredited institution after graduation. Visit the organization's Web site for more information.

Scholarship America
4960 Viking Drive, Suite 110
Edina, MN 55435-5314
800-279-2083
http://www.scholarshipamerica.org

This organization works through its local Dollars for Scholars chapters throughout the United States. To date, it has awarded more than $1 billion in scholarships to more than one million students. Visit Scholarship America's Web site for more information.

Scholarships.com
http://www.scholarships.com

Scholarships.com offers a free college scholarship search engine (although you must register to use it) and financial aid information. Its awards database features 3,000 listings worth up to $3 billion in aid.

Sphinx Organization
400 Renaissance Center, Suite 2550
Detroit, MI 48243-1679
313-877-9100
info@sphinxmusic.org
http://www.sphinxmusic.org

This organization, which promotes diversity in classical education, offers a variety of competitions for young classical musicians. Awards range from $2,000 to $10,000. Contact the Sphinx Organization for more information.

Texas Music Teachers Association
1106 Clayton Lane 240W
Austin, TX 78723-1066
512-419-1352
tmta@tmta.org
http://tmta.org/whitlock_memorial_
   scholarships.htm

Texas high school students with musical ability may apply for the Whitlock Memorial Scholarship Award, which ranges from $50 to $915 depending on funding. Potential applicants should contact the association or their local music teacher for additional eligibility requirements.

United Negro College Fund (UNCF)

8260 Willow Oaks Corporate Drive
PO Box 10444
Fairfax, VA 22031-8044
http://www.uncf.org/scholarships/
   index.asp

Visitors to the UNCF Web site can search for thousands of scholarships and grants, many of which are administered by the UNCF. High school seniors and undergraduate and graduate students are eligible. The search engine allows you to search by major (such as advertising, business, education, music, and the performing arts), state, scholarship title, grade level, and achievement score.

Young Musicians Foundation

195 South Beverly Drive, Suite 414
Beverly Hills, CA 90212-3044
310-859-7668
info@ymf.org
http://www.ymf.org/programs/
   scholarship.php

The foundation provides music education scholarships to instrumentalists through their senior year in high school and to vocalists through age 25. Applicants must demonstrate exceptional talent and financial need and be residents of Southern California. Awards range from $250 to $3,000. Visit the foundation's Web site for details and to download an application.

Look to the Pros

The following professional organizations offer a variety of materials, from career brochures to lists of accredited schools to salary surveys. Many of them also publish journals and newsletters that you should become familiar with. Some also have annual conferences that you might be able to attend. (While you may not be able to attend a conference as a participant, it may be possible to "cover" one for your school or even your local paper, especially if your school has a related club.)

When contacting professional organizations, keep in mind that all exist primarily to serve their members, be it through continuing education, professional licensure, political lobbying, or just "keeping up with the profession." While many are strongly interested in promoting their profession and passing information about it to the general public, these busy professional organizations are not there solely to provide you with information. Whether you call or write, be courteous, brief, and to the point. Know what you need and ask for it. If the organization has a Web site, check it out first: what you're looking for may be available there for downloading, or you may find a list of prices or instructions, such as sending a self-addressed stamped envelope with your request. Finally, be aware that organizations, like people, move. To save time when writing, first confirm the address, preferably with a quick phone call to the organization itself, "Hello, I'm calling to confirm your address. . ."

❏ THE SOURCES

American Association of University Professors

1012 14th Street, NW, Suite 500
Washington, DC 20005-3406
202-737-5900
http://www.aaup.org

Contact the association for information about earnings and union membership for college professors.

American Federation of Musicians of the United States and Canada

1501 Broadway, Suite 600
New York, NY 10036-5505
212-869-1330
http://www.afm.org

This union represents the interests of professional musicians. Its Web site provides a wealth of information on the music industry and careers, a searchable database of U.S. and foreign music schools, and links to scholarships.

American Federation of Teachers (AFT)

555 New Jersey Avenue, NW
Washington, DC 20001-2029
202-879-4400
online@aft.org
http://www.aft.org

The AFT is a professional membership organization for teachers (including music teachers) at all levels. In addition to membership benefits, the federation offers information on important issues affecting educators, salary surveys, and useful periodicals.

American Guild of Musical Artists (AGMA)

1430 Broadway, 14th Floor
New York, NY 10018-3308
212-265-3687
AGMA@musicalartists.org
http://www.musicalartists.org

The AGMA is a union for professional musicians. Its Web site lists upcoming auditions, news about the field, and membership information.

American Guild of Organists (AGO)

475 Riverside Drive, Suite 1260
New York, NY 10115-0055
212-870-2310
info@agohq.org
http://www.agohq.org

The AGO represents the professional interests of organists. Visit its Web site to read *A Young Person's Guide to the Organ*.

American Music Therapy Association

8455 Colesville Road, Suite 1000
Silver Spring, MD 20910-3392
301-589-3300
info@musictherapy.org
http://www.musictherapy.org

Visit the association's Web site for comprehensive information about the career of music therapist, a list of approved educational programs, and details on internships and membership for college students.

American Musicological Society Inc.

Bowdoin College
6010 College Station
Brunswick, ME 04011-8451
207-798-4243
ams@ams-net.org
http://www.ams-net.org

Visit the society's Web site for a list of graduate programs in musicology and information on awards, grants, and fellowships.

American Society of Composers, Authors, and Publishers (ASCAP)

One Lincoln Plaza
New York, NY 10023-7129
212-621-6000
info@ascap.com
http://www.ascap.com

ASCAP is a membership association of U.S. composers, songwriters, lyricists, and music publishers in all genres of music.

Visit its Web site for membership information and useful articles on the music industry.

American String Teachers Association

4153 Chain Bridge Road
Fairfax, VA 22030-4102
703-279-2113
asta@astaweb.com
http://www.astaweb.com

This organization represents the professional interests of teachers of stringed instruments. Visit its Web site for information on stringed instruments, membership for college students, and competitions. The association also offers a separate Web site, http://www.career-sinstringteaching.com, which features detailed information on careers in the field, educational options, and summer camps. A mentorship program and an online chat room are also available.

American Symphony Orchestra League

33 West 60th Street, 5th Floor
New York, NY 10023-7905
212-262-5161
league@symphony.org
http://www.symphony.org

Visit the league's Web site for information on conducting fellowships, orchestra management careers, information interviews, and job listings.

Audio Engineering Society

60 East 42nd Street, Room 2520
New York, NY 10165-2520
212-661-8528

HQ@aes.org
http://www.aes.org

Contact the society for information on graduate-level scholarships, a list of audio recording schools and courses in the United States and abroad, grants for graduate study, and membership for college students.

Broadcast Education Association (BEA)

1771 N Street, NW
Washington, DC 20036-2891
888-380-7222
beainfo@beaweb.org
http://www.beaweb.org

An association of university broadcasting faculty, industry professionals, and graduate students, BEA offers annual scholarships in broadcasting for college juniors, seniors, and graduate students. Visit its Web site for useful information about broadcast education and the broadcasting industry.

Broadcast Music Inc. (BMI)

320 West 57th Street
New York, NY 10019-3790
212-586-2000
newyork@bmi.com
http://www.bmi.com

BMI is a performing rights organization that represents songwriters, composers, and music publishers in all types of music. Visit the Songwriter's section of its Web site to learn more about performing rights, music publishing, copyright, and the business of songwriting.

Certification Board for Music Therapists

506 East Lancaster Avenue, Suite 102
Downingtown, PA 19335-2776
800-765-2268
info@cbmt.org
http://www.cbmt.org

Visit the board's Web site for information on certification for music therapists.

The College Music Society (CMS)

312 East Pine Street
Missoula, MT 59802-4624
406-721-9616
cms@music.org
http://www.music.org

The CMS is a consortium of college, university, conservatory, and independent musicians and scholars interested in all aspects of music and music teaching. Visit its Web site for a directory of U.S. and Canadian music programs, statistics on music education, and information on membership for college students.

Conductors' Guild Inc.

5300 Glenside Drive, Suite 2207
Richmond, VA 23228-3983
804-553-1378
guild@conductorsguild.net
http://www.conductorsguild.org

The guild represents the professional interests of music conductors. Visit its Web site for information on membership for college students and its mentoring program for young conductors.

Directors Guild of America (DGA)

7920 Sunset Boulevard
Los Angeles, CA 90046-3304
310-289-2000
http://www.dga.org

Visit the guild's Web site to learn more about the industry and DGA-sponsored training programs and to read selected articles from *DGA Magazine.*

MENC: The National Association for Music Education

1806 Robert Fulton Drive
Reston, VA 20191-5462
800-336-3768
http://www.menc.org

To participate in online forums about music education and to read a variety of useful online brochures, such as *Careers in Music* and *How to Nail a College Entrance Audition,* visit MENC's Web site. The association also offers membership to college students and an honor society for middle and high school music students.

Music & Entertainment Industry Educators Association

1900 Belmont Boulevard
Nashville, TN 37212-3757
615-460-6946
office@meiea.org
http://www.meiea.org

The primary goal of this association is to "facilitate an exchange of information between educators and practitioners in order to prepare students for careers in the music and entertainment industries." Visit its Web site to read free e-zines, participate in a Web forum, and access a list of schools that offer degrees in music-related fields.

Music Library Association

8551 Research Way, Suite 180
Middleton, WI 53562-3567
608-836-5825
http://www.musiclibraryassoc.org

Visit the association's Web site for information on membership for college students; to read *Music Librarianship: Is it for you?*, a useful career publication; and to access an online version of the *Directory of Library School Offerings in Music Librarianship*.

Music Teachers National Association

441 Vine Street, Suite 505
Cincinnati, OH 45202-2813
888-512-5278
mtnanet@mtna.org
http://www.mtna.org

Visit the association's Web site for information on competitions, membership for college students, choosing a music teacher, and certification.

Music Video Production Association

201 North Occidental Street
Los Angeles, CA 90026-4603
213-387-1590
info@mvpa.com
http://www.mvpa.com

This organization offers training seminars and other resources to music video professionals.

National Academy of Recording Arts and Sciences (NARAS)

3402 Pico Boulevard
Santa Monica, CA 90405-2118
310-392-3777
http://grammy.com

Visit the NARAS Web site to read about efforts to support the recording industry and to check out links to music- and recording-related sites.

National Association of Composers, USA

PO Box 49256, Barrington Station
Los Angeles, CA 90049-0256
310-541-8213
nacusa@music-usa.org
http://www.music-usa.org/nacusa

The association offers an annual young composer's competition and other contests. Visit its Web site for details.

National Association of Schools of Music (NASM)

11250 Roger Bacon Drive, Suite 21
Reston, VA 20190-5248
703-437-0700
info@arts-accredit.org
http://nasm.arts-accredit.org

The NASM is an association of schools of music, mainly at the college level, but also including precollegiate and community schools of music. Contact the NASM for information on accredited music programs. You can search a free online version of its list of accredited institutions by name, city, and/or state. (For a small fee, you can search a more extensive version of the list.) Additionally, visit the FAQ:

Students, Parents, Public section for useful information on preparing to study music in college, applying for financial aid, and accreditation.

National Council for Accreditation of Teacher Education (NCATE)

2010 Massachusetts Avenue, NW, Suite 500
Washington, DC 20036-1012
202-466-7496
ncate@ncate.org
http://www.ncate.org

Visit the council's Web site to read the following resources: FAQs About Careers in Education, What to Look for in a Teacher Preparation Program?, and Why Attend an NCATE-Accredited College of Education?

National Endowment for the Arts (NEA)

Arts and Education
Education and Access Division
Nancy Hanks Center
1100 Pennsylvania Avenue, NW
Washington, DC 20506-0001
202-682-5400
http://arts.endow.gov

Established by Congress in 1965 to support excellence in the arts, the NEA offers grants to artists and arts organizations, as well as various community-based programs. Visit its Web site for more information.

Opera America

330 Seventh Avenue, 16th Floor
New York, NY 10001-5010
212-796-8620
frontdesk@operaamerica.org
http://www.operaamerica.org

Visit this organization's Web site for career and educational information for opera singers and a list of recommended reading, listening, and Web sites for K-12 students who are interested in opera.

Recording Industry Association of America (RIAA)

1330 Connecticut Avenue, NW, Suite 300
Washington, DC 20036-1725
202-775-0101
http://www.riaa.com

The RIAA is a trade organization that represents the U.S. recording industry. Visit its Web site for facts and statistics about the industry.

Society for Ethnomusicology

1165 East 3rd Street
Morrison Hall 005
Indiana University
Bloomington, IN 47405-3700
sem@indiana.edu
http://www.ethnomusicology.org

According to the society, the field of ethnomusicology "explores human music-making activities all over the world, in all styles, from the immediate present to the distant past." Visit its Web site for more information on the field, fellowships, and links to ethnomusicology degree programs.

Society of Broadcast Engineers

9247 North Meridian Street, Suite 150

Indianapolis, IN 46260-1976
317-846-9000
mclappe@sbe.org
http://www.sbe.org

Visit the society's Web site for information on membership for high school and college students, scholarships, certification, education programs, and professional publications.

Society of Professional Audio Recording Services

9 Music Square South, Suite 222
Nashville, TN 37203-3211
800-771-7727
spars@spars.com
http://www.spars.com

This organization represents the professional interests of audio recording professionals.

Songwriters Guild of America

1500 Harbor Boulevard
Weehawken, NJ 07086-6732
201-867-7603
songwritersnj@aol.com
http://www.songwritersguild.com

The guild represents the professional interests of songwriters. It offers a membership option to beginning songwriters. Visit its Web site for more information.

Sphinx Organization

400 Renaissance Center, Suite 2550
Detroit, MI 48243-1679
313-877-9100
info@sphinxmusic.org
http://www.sphinxmusic.org

The Sphinx Organization seeks to encourage young minority musicians to pursue classical music. Its Web site offers information on competitions, scholarships, and educational programs.

Women Band Directors National Association

296 Dailey Hills Circle
Ringgold, GA 30736-8156
http://www.womenbanddirectors.org

This organization represents the professional interests of female band directors. Visit its Web site for information on scholarships and membership for high school and college students.

Women In Music—National Network

PO Box 1925
El Cerrito, CA 94530-4925
866-305-7963
admin@womeninmusic.com
http://www.womeninmusic.com

This organization offers information on networking opportunities, detailed career information, membership, and a mentoring program for women in music at its Web site.

Young Musicians Foundation

195 South Beverly Drive, Suite 414
Beverly Hills, CA 90212-3044
310-859-7668
info@ymf.org
http://www.ymf.org

The foundation offers a wealth of educational programs, competitions, camps, and other resources to young musicians in Southern California. Visit its Web site for more information.

Index

Entries and page numbers in **bold** indicate major treatment of a topic.

A